THE SHADOW EFFECT

The
Shadow
Effect

Illuminating the Hidden Power of Your True Self

Deepak CHOPRA
Debbie FORD
Marianne WILLIAMSON

HarperOne
An Imprint of HarperCollinsPublishers

HarperOne

HarperCollins books may be purchased for educational, business, or sales promotional use. For information please write: Special Markets Department, HarperCollins Publishers, 10 East 53rd Street, New York, NY 10022.

HarperCollins website: http://www.harpercollins.com

HarperCollins®, ▉®, and HarperOne™
are trademarks of HarperCollins Publishers

FIRST HARPERCOLLINS PAPERBACK EDITION PUBLISHED IN 2011
Designed by Level C

Library of Congress Cataloging-in-Publication Data
The shadow effect : illuminating the hidden power of your true self /
by Deepak Chopra, Debbie Ford, Marianne Williamson. — 1st ed.
p. cm.
ISBN 978–0–06–196264–6
1. Subconsciousness. 2. Psychology. I. Ford, Debbie.
II. Williamson, Marianne. III. Title.
BF315.C53   2010
154.2—dc22   2010003787

12 13 14 15   RRD(H)   10 9 8 7 6 5 4 3

Contents

Introduction

The conflict between who we are and who we want to be is at the core of the human struggle. Duality, in fact, lies at the very center of the human experience. Life and death, good and evil, hope and resignation coexist in every person and exert their force in every facet of our lives. If we know courage, it is because we have also experienced fear; if we can recognize honesty, it is because we have encountered deceit. And yet most of us deny or ignore our dualistic nature.

If we are living under the assumption that we are only one way or another, inside a limited spectrum of human qualities, then we would have to question why more of us aren't wholly satisfied with our lives right now. Why do we have access to so much wisdom yet fail to have the strength and courage to act upon our good intentions by making powerful choices? And most important, why do we continue to act out in ways that go against our value system and all that we stand for? We will assert that it is because of our unexamined life, our darker self, our shadow self where our unclaimed power lies hidden. It is here, in this least likely place, that we will find the key to unlock our strength, our happiness, and our ability to live out our dreams.

We have been conditioned to fear the shadow side of life and the shadow side of ourselves. When we catch ourselves thinking a dark thought or acting out in a behavior that we feel is unacceptable, we run, just like a groundhog, back into our hole and hide, hoping, praying, it will disappear before we venture out again. Why do we do this? Because we are afraid that no matter how hard we try, we will never be able to escape from this part of ourselves. And although ignoring or repressing our dark side is the norm, the sobering truth is that running from the shadow only intensifies its power. Denying it only leads to more pain, suffering, regret, and resignation. If we fail to take responsibility and extract the wisdom that has been hidden beneath the surface of our conscious minds, the shadow will take charge, and instead of us being able to have control over it, the shadow winds up having control over us, triggering the shadow effect. Our dark side then starts making our decisions for us, stripping us of our right to make conscious choices whether it's what food we will eat, how much money we will spend, or what addiction we will succumb to. Our shadow incites us to act out in ways we never imagined we could and to waste our vital energy on bad habits and repetitive behaviors. Our shadow keeps us from full self-expression, from speaking our truth, and from living an authentic life. It is only by embracing our duality that we free ourselves of the behaviors that can potentially bring us down. If we don't acknowledge all of who we are, we are guaranteed to be blindsided by the shadow effect.

The shadow effect is everywhere. Evidence of its pervasiveness can be seen in every aspect of our lives. We read about it online. We watch it on the nightly news, and we can see it in our friends, our family, and strangers on the street. And perhaps most significant, we can recognize it in our thoughts, see it in our behaviors, and feel it in our interactions with others. We worry that shining a light on this darkness will cause us to feel great shame or, even worse, to act out our worst nightmare. We become scared of what we will find if we look inside ourselves, so instead we bury our heads and refuse to face our shadow sides.

But this book reveals a new truth—shared from three life-changing perspectives—that the opposite of what we fear we will experience is what actually occurs. Instead of shame, we feel compassion. Instead of embarrassment, we gain courage. Instead of limitation, we experience freedom. If left unopened, the shadow is a Pandora's box filled with secrets that we fear will destroy everything we love and care about. But if we open the box, we discover that what's inside has the power to radically and *positively* alter our lives. Then we will step out of the illusion that our darkness will overtake us and instead we will see the world in a new light. The compassion we discover for ourselves will ignite our confidence and courage as we open our hearts to those around us. The power we unearth will help us tackle the fear that has been holding us back and will urge us to move powerfully toward our highest potential. Far from frightening, embracing the shadow allows us to be whole, to be real, to take back our power, to unleash our passion, and to realize our dreams.

This book was born out of a desire to illuminate the many life-altering gifts of the shadow. In the following pages, each of us will approach the subject from our own unique perspective as teachers. Our intention is to provide a comprehensive, multi-lens understanding of how the shadow was born within us, how it functions in our lives, and most important, what we can do to discover the gifts of our true nature. We promise that after reading this book you will never think of your shadow self in the same way again.

In Part I, Deepak Chopra gives us a comprehensive overview of our dualistic nature and offers a prescription to return us to wholeness. A mind/body pioneer, Chopra has transformed millions of lives with his teachings. His holistic approach to the divisive nature of the shadow is both grounding and illuminating.

In Part II, I draw upon nearly fifteen years of teaching and leading The Shadow Process around the world to offer an accessible yet in-depth examination of the birth of the shadow, the role of the shadow in our everyday lives, and how we can reclaim the power and brilliance of our authentic nature.

In Part III, Marianne Williamson touches our hearts and minds with a provocative exploration of the connection between the shadow and the soul. A renowned international spiritual teacher, Marianne takes our hand and guides us through the bumpy terrain of the battle between love and fear.

Each of us comes with years of experience and a sincere hope that we can illuminate the shadow once and for all. For if we do not counter the force of the shadow and integrate its wisdom, it has the potential to continue to wreak havoc on our lives and our world. When we fail to admit to our vulnerabilities and recognize our bad behaviors, we will inevitably sabotage ourselves when we are on the verge of some personal or professional breakthrough. Then the shadow wins. When we act out of disproportionate anger in speaking to our children, the shadow wins. When we deceive our loved ones, the shadow wins. When we refuse to accept our true nature, the shadow wins. If we do not bring the light of our highest self to the darkness of our human impulses, the shadow wins. Until we accept all of who we are, the shadow effect will have the power to impede our happiness. If left unacknowledged, the shadow will stop us from being whole, prevent us from achieving our best-laid plans, and leave us living half a life. It is our hope in writing this book that we will bring the shadow into the light. There has never been a better time to create a new lexicon, to illuminate the shadow, and to finally understand what's been so difficult to see and hard to explain.

Shadow work, as described in this book, is more than a psychological process or an intellectual banter. It is a prescriptive solution to problems unsolved. It is a life-altering journey that goes beyond any psychological theory because it deems the dark side as a human issue, a spiritual issue that all of us must resolve in this lifetime if we are to live a fully self-expressed life. We will finally understand why we are no better and no worse than anyone else regardless of our color, our background, our sexual orientation, our genetic makeup, or our past. There is no one in the world who doesn't have a shadow, and when taken seriously and understood, the shadow can birth a new reality that will alter the way we feel about ourselves, the way we parent our children, the way we treat our partners, the way we interact with our community members, and the way we engage with other nations.

I believe that the shadow is one of the greatest gifts available to us. Carl Jung called it a "sparring partner"; it is the opponent within us that exposes our flaws and sharpens our skills. It is the teacher, the trainer, and the guide that supports us in uncovering our true magnificence. The shadow is not a problem to be solved or an enemy to be conquered but a fertile field to be cultivated. When we dig our hands into its rich soil, we will discover the potent seeds of the people we most desire to be. It is our sincere hope that you take this journey, for we know what's waiting inside.

Debbie Ford

PART

I

The Shadow

DEEPAK CHOPRA

Once people hear about the shadow, the dark side of human nature, almost no one denies that it exists. Every life has been touched by anger and fear. The evening news exposes human nature at its worst, week after week, without letup. If we are honest with ourselves, dark impulses are free to roam our minds at will, and the price we pay for being a good person—something we all aspire to—is that the bad person who might ruin everything must be kept under wraps.

Having a shadow side seems to call for some kind of intervention, maybe therapy or a pill, maybe a trip to the confessional or a midnight soul confrontation. As soon as people acknowledge that they have it, they want to be rid of it. There are many aspects of life in which a can-do, let's-fix-it attitude works. Unfortunately, the shadow isn't one of them. The reason that the shadow hasn't been fixed for thousands of years—the whole time that human beings have been conscious of their dark side—is totally mysterious. It only makes sense to unravel the mystery before asking how to deal with it. Therefore, I've divided Part I into three sections, in which I fall back on a physician's instinct to find a diagnosis, offer a cure, and then honestly tell patients their prognosis for the future:

The Fog of Illusion

The Way Out

A New Reality, a New Power

The first section (the diagnosis) describes how the shadow came to be. I differ from some in believing that the shadow is a human creation, not a cosmic force or a universal curse. The second section (the cure) deals with how you can diminish the shadow's hidden power over you in everyday life. The third section (the prognosis) unfolds a future in which the shadow has been dismantled, not only for certain individuals, but for all of us. Together we created the shadow that now haunts us. Despite our fear and reluctance to face this fact, it turns out to be the key to transformation. If you and I weren't part of the problem, we would have no hope of being part of the solution.

THE FOG OF ILLUSION

If you cannot see your own shadow, you must go in search of it. The shadow hides in shame in the dark alleys, secret passages, and ghost-filled attics of your consciousness. To have a shadow is not to be flawed, but to be complete. That's a hard truth to confront. (Haven't you tried to tell people a candid truth about themselves, only to have them snap back, "Don't psychoanalyze me," or something of the sort? The unconscious realm feels as dangerous as the depths of the ocean; both are dark and full of unseen monsters.) We are all living with the wreckage of failed ideals that once seemed like perfect solutions. Each solution matches a picture of what the dark side is all about.

If you think that shadow aspects like fear, anger, anxiety, and violence are the result of demonic possession, the solution is to purify the afflicted person. Demons can be driven out with rituals, cleansing of the body, fasting, and grueling austerities. This is not a primitive notion. Millions of modern people hold fast to it. You can't pass a newsstand without seeing a glossy magazine that promises a new you through some kind of purification, whether it's a diet that will overcome your craving for bad foods or a checklist for finding the right spouse by avoiding the wrong types of people. "Clean up your act" is the modern version of purifying from demons.

Akin to this explanation is the notion that cosmic evil has been loosed in the world. If this is your explanation for the shadow, the natural solution is religion. Religion aligns you with cosmic good in its battle against cosmic evil. For millions of people this war is very real. It extends to every aspect of their lives, from sexual temptation to abortion, the rise of godless atheism, and the decline of patriotism. The Devil creates every form of human suffering and wrongdoing. Only God (or the gods) has the power to defeat Satan and redeem us from sin. Yet it's hard to settle whether religion defeats the shadow or actually makes it stronger by arousing strong feelings of sinfulness and guilt, shame and fear about the tortures of a hellish hereafter.

Since we pride ourselves on living in an age when superstition no longer rules our lives, these time-honored explanations of the dark side are no longer the only choices. People can turn their backs on cosmic evil and take personal responsibility. The dark side has been updated as sickness, a branch of mental health. Along this path lies a huge array of treatments. Addicts are sent into recovery programs. The anxious and depressed are sent to psychiatrists. Out-of-control rage-aholics wind up in anger-management classes after ramming a car on the freeway when they can't control themselves.

Given all these explanations, each of which leads to a definite solution, why is the shadow undefeated?

This may seem like a gloomy prospect, but in fact the first step toward dealing with the shadow is to acknowledge its power. Human nature includes a self-destructive side. When Swiss psychologist Carl Jung posited the archetype of the shadow, he said that it creates a fog of illusion that surrounds the self. Trapped in this fog, we evade our own darkness, and thus we give the shadow more and more power over us. It's no secret that the Jungian approach to archetypes quickly turns very intellectual and complicated. But the stubborn power of the shadow isn't complex at all. I flicked on the television while taking a break from writing this paragraph. The famous billionaire Warren Buffett was being interviewed about booms and busts in the economic cycle.

"Do you think there will be another bubble leading to a huge recession?" the interviewer asked.

"I can guarantee it," Buffett replied.

The interviewer shook his head. "Why can't we learn the lessons of the last recession? Look where greed has gotten us."

Buffett gave a small mysterious smile. "Greed is fun for a while. People can't resist it. However far human beings have come, we haven't grown emotionally at all. We remain the same."

In capsule form, there's the shadow and the problems it poses. In the fog of illusion, we don't see our worst impulses as self-destructive. They're irresistible, even fun. Hence the enormous popularity of revenge dramas as entertainment, whether in Shakespeare's theater or a spaghetti Western on the silver screen. What could be better than unleashing all our hidden rage, demolishing the enemy, and walking tall in triumph? The shadow exerts its power by making the darkness seem like the light.

The world's wisdom traditions have spent most of their energy and thought meeting the same primal dilemmas. Creation has a dark side. Destruction is inherent in nature. Death interrupts life. Decay saps vitality. Evil is attractive. No wonder the fog of illusion eventually seems like a nice place to be. If you face reality head-on, the dark side is too overwhelming to bear. Yet there is a counterforce that has steadily—and successfully—overcome the dark side. The wreckage of failed solutions keeps us from seeing it. The fog of illusion insulates us from it. You would never guess, dialing past the disasters and horrors of nightly television, that human beings have always had the power to find peace, exaltation, and freedom from darkness.

The secret lies in the word "consciousness." When people hear this, a look of disappointment crosses their faces. Consciousness is old hat. We've heard about consciousness-raising ever since feminism appeared, along with other varieties of liberation. Higher consciousness is held out as a promise by countless spiritual movements. You might even be tempted to throw consciousness onto the pile of wrecked ideals, because in the face of sincere attempts to raise our consciousness, the shadow plagues the world with war, crime, and violence, just as it plagues individual lives with pain and fear.

We have come to a crossroads. Either consciousness belongs with the other false answers, or it hasn't been tried in the right way. I'd like to suggest that the latter is true. Higher consciousness is the answer—the only lasting answer—to the dark side of human nature. It's not the answer that's at fault here—it's the application. There are countless paths to healing the soul, just as there are countless alternative treatments for cancer. But no one has enough time and energy to experiment with all of them. It's vital to pick a path that takes you where you want to go. For that to happen, a much deeper analysis of the shadow is required. If you approach the darkness superficially, it will always persist, because the shadow isn't as simple an enemy as sickness, a demon, or a cosmic devil. It's an aspect of reality so basic to creation that only complete understanding can successfully confront it.

The Truth of One Reality

The first step in defeating the shadow is to abandon all notions of defeating it. The dark side of human nature thrives on war, struggle, and conflict. As soon as you talk about "winning," you have lost already. You have been dragged into the duality of good and evil. Once that happens, nothing can end the duality. Good has no power to defeat its opposite once and for all. I know that this is hard to accept. In each of our lives there are past actions we are ashamed of and present impulses we fight against. All around us are acts of unspeakable violence. War and crime devastate whole societies. People desperately pray to a higher power that can restore light where darkness prevails.

Realists long ago gave up hope of seeing the good side of human nature overcome the bad. The life of Sigmund Freud, one of the most realistic thinkers who ever confronted the psyche, came to a close as the raging violence of Nazism devoured Europe. He had concluded that civilization exists at a tragic cost. We must repress our wild, atavistic instincts in order to keep them in check, and yet despite our best efforts there will be many defeats. The world erupts in mass violence; individuals erupt in personal violence. This analysis implies a terrible kind of resignation. The "good me" has no chance of living a peaceful, loving, orderly life unless the "bad me" is shoved down into the darkness and caged in solitary confinement.

Realists will concede that repression itself is an evil. If you try to smother your feelings of anger, fear, insecurity, jealousy, and sexuality, the shadow gains more energy for its own use. And that use is ruthless. When the dark side turns on you, havoc reigns.

Last week I had a call from a woman who was desperately seeking a place of shelter and safety. Her abusive husband was a chronic alcoholic. They had been dealing with the problem for years. After periods of sobriety he would relapse and go on long benders that disrupted work and family, leaving him exhausted and ashamed when they came to an end. He had recently disappeared for a week, and this time when he came back all his remorse and contrition fell on deaf ears. His wife wanted out. The husband's reaction was to turn violent. He struck her, which she said had never happened before. Now in addition to all her frustration and tears she was afraid for her own safety.

In the short run, all one can do is hand out the best advice about shelters and women's support groups. But as I hung up, feeling in myself the residue of her shattered emotions, I thought about the long run. Addicts who relapse have become a standard feature of the psychological landscape. But what do they really represent? I think they are an extreme example of a common situation: a divided self. For addicts, the separation between the "good me" and the "bad me" cannot be resolved. Normally, the tactics for dealing with one's dark side come rather easily. It's not hard to deny your bad deeds, forget your wicked impulses, apologize for getting angry, and show contrition for your misdeeds. Addicts cannot settle for these easy prescriptions. Their darker impulses preoccupy them without the normal checks and restraints. Even access to simple pleasure is denied. The demons inside undermine pleasure and spoil it; they mock happiness; they remind addicts repeatedly of their weakness and badness.

Let's say that this description is roughly correct. I have left out some important ingredients. Habit plays a strong part in addiction. So do physical changes in the brain—substance abusers have attacked the receptors in the brain using alien chemicals that in time destroy the normal responses of pleasure and pain. Yet these physical aspects of addiction have been grossly overstated. If addiction was primarily physical, then millions of people wouldn't be casually using alcohol and drugs. Yet they do, with relatively little long-term harm and minimal chance of addiction. Without entering the heated controversy over addiction and its causes, one can step back and see it not as an isolated problem, but as yet another expression of the shadow.

Therefore, to treat addictions, we must approach the shadow and disarm it. Since all of us want to do just that, let me stay with the drunken husband returning from a weeklong bender. He will stand in for other expressions of the shadow, such as a violent temper, racial prejudice, sexual chauvinism, and much more. These may not seem to be related at first glance. A boss who practices sexual harassment isn't displaying the same out-of-control behavior of a gay basher committing a hate crime. Yet the shadow provides a common link. Whenever any aspect of the self has been split off, labeled as bad, illicit, shameful, guilty, or wrong, the shadow gains power. It doesn't matter whether the dark side of human nature expresses itself in utmost violence or in mild, socially tolerated ways. The essential fact is that a part of the self has been split off.

Once split off, the fragment that is "bad" loses touch with the central core of the self, the part we consider "good" because of its seeming lack of violence, anger, and fear. This is the adult self, the ego that has adapted well to the world and other people. The drunken husband has a good self, of course. He could have a much nicer and more acceptable good self than normal. The more you repress your dark side, the easier it is to construct a persona that shines with goodness and light. (Hence the repeated surprise of neighbors who tell the TV crews, in the aftermath of a mass shooting spree or other hideous crime, that the perpetrator "seemed like such a nice man.")

I knew from talking to the distraught wife that her husband had been in and out of rehab. Sometimes the treatment worked for a while. But even during his sober periods, the man was miserable. He was constantly on guard lest the monkey jump on his back again. He feared his next relapse, yet as hard as he fought against it, the prospect was inevitable. Even during a time of temporary victory, the shadow had only to watch and wait.

One time when her husband was in the throes of the DTs, his night sweats and delirium became unbearable. The wife fled to a doctor, begging for a drug that would quell his symptoms. But she happened to hit upon a doctor who was a stubborn realist, and he refused. "Let him hit rock bottom," he said. "That's his only real hope. Short of that, you won't be helping him by making this less painful."

You and I might think of this as callous advice. But the phenomenon of hitting rock bottom is well known in addiction circles. It can pose a terrible risk, because when the shadow's bluff is called, it resorts to extremes of self-destruction. There is no practical limit to how much suffering the unconscious can create, and we are all fragile. Addicts—or any in the grip of shadow energies—are trapped in a fog of illusion. Inside that fog, nothing exists but craving and the terror of not getting a fix.

When the perilous journey of hitting rock bottom works, the reason is that this fog clears. The addict begins to have thoughts that are actually realistic: "I am more than my addiction. I don't want to lose everything. Fear can be overcome. It's time for this to end." In such moments of clarity, the power of healing comes from the clarity itself. The person smashes through the allure of self-destruction and sees how irrational it is. In clarity the self comes together and sees itself without blinders.

You have only one self. It is the real you. It is beyond good and evil.

The shadow loses its power when consciousness stops being divided. When you are no longer split, there's nothing to see but one self in all directions. There are no hidden compartments, dungeons, torture cells, or mossy rocks to hide under. Consciousness sees itself. That is its most basic function, but, as we will discover, from this simple function a new self and eventually a new world can be born.

The Collective Shadow

Jung's naming of the shadow wasn't his major achievement; neither was his theory of archetypes. His major achievement was to show that human beings share a self. "Who am I?" depends on "Who are we?" Human beings are the only creatures who can create a self. In fact, we must create one, because the self gives us a point of view, a unique focus on the world. Without a self, our brains would be bombarded with a bewildering flood of sensory images that would not make sense. Infants lack a self and spend the first three years creating it, fashioning their personalities and preferences, temperaments and interests. Every mother can testify that the time her baby spends as a blank slate is minimal, if it exists at all. We enter the world not as passive receivers of sense data, but as eager creators. Once you become a single self with needs, beliefs, impulses, drives, wishes, dreams, and fears, suddenly the world makes sense. "I, me, and mine" exists for one purpose, to give you a personal stake in the world.

We all have a self, and we go to great lengths to defend its right to exist. But our creation is fragile. We have all experienced personal crises, such as the sudden death of a loved one or the discovery that we are seriously ill. Any crisis that attacks our sense of well-being also attacks our sense of self. If you lose your house or all your money or your spouse, this external event sends tremors of fear and doubt throughout the self. At any moment when you feel that your world is falling apart, what is really falling apart is the self and its confidence that it understands reality. After any major trauma to body or mind, it takes time for the fragile ego-personality to recover. (We are very lucky that an old adage is true: "Souls don't break; they bounce.")

Because we don't know how we created the self that we cling to so desperately, the self can surprise and amaze us. Freud sprang a major surprise when he said that the self has a hidden dimension filled with drives and desires that we hardly recognize. After becoming Freud's most prominent disciple, Jung realized that his mentor had made a mistake. The unconscious isn't about me. It's about us. When a person has unconscious impulses and drives, they come from the entire history of humankind. Each of us, according to Jung, is linked to a "collective unconscious," as he called it. The notion that you and I created our separate, isolated selves is an illusion. We tapped into the vast reservoir of all human aspirations, drives, and myths. This shared unconscious is also where the shadow lives.

Some people are social, others asocial, but no one can stand outside the collective self. "We" is a constant reminder that no man is an island. Jung peeled away the social surface to expose the hidden dimension of "we." Calling this realm the collective unconscious made it sound more technical, perhaps, but the self you and I share with everyone else is basic to our survival. Think of the ways you fall back on the collective self. Here are just a few:

When you need the support of your family and closest friends

When you join a political party

When you volunteer for a charity or a community

When you choose to fight for your country or otherwise defend it

When you identify with your nationality

When you think in terms of "us versus them"

When a disaster somewhere else affects you personally

When you are gripped by collective fear

It's a fantasy to believe that you can opt out of "we," even though all of us try to. We want to be seen as Americans but not the Ugly American. We sympathize with other ethnic groups but also feel different, separate, and usually better. In a crisis we want our families as close as possible, yet on other occasions we insist on being individuals with a life outside the family. The coalition between "I" and "we" is an uneasy one.

Jung made it even more uneasy. When it comes to the collective shadow, people struggle to opt out. (Society will never stop moving in ways we disapprove of.) But this is actually harder than opting out of a family role; indeed, the family is only the first unit or level of the collective self, the one we tend to see fairly easily. At Thanksgiving you can announce that you've changed, that you don't deserve to be treated like a spoiled five-year-old or rebellious teenager. You may not feel that you are being heard. Your family may have too much invested in keeping you inside your old box. Society, however, is even harsher and less understanding.

Society has its invisible hooks in all of us. You can become a pacifist in times of war. That's an individual choice. Yet it doesn't automatically extract you from the collective shadow, where war is born out of rage, prejudice, resentment, old grievances, and the dark underbelly of nationalism. Perhaps the discredited term of "racial memory" is viable, even though it makes us feel extremely uncomfortable. Yet millions of people aren't uncomfortable making statements like "a typical male response" or "women drivers." Gender has turned into a hotly contested allegiance. The collective unconscious has you entangled at this moment. On the surface Citizen X may be wildly opposed to Citizen Y, but at the unconscious level they are conjoined, like the two ends of a tug-of-war.

The choice to opt in or opt out becomes the central issue of the collective shadow. It gives rise to many questions in everyday life:

What is my social obligation?

What is my patriotic duty?

How much should I conform to or resist society?

How connected am I to other people?

What do I owe to the less fortunate?

Can I change the world?

Asking any of these questions, your conscious mind cannot give the whole answer—or even the truest answer. Beneath the surface, the collective unconscious is roiling with drives, prejudices, frustrated desires, fears, and memories that are part of you because "we" is your identity as much as "I."

Where's the Proof?

For a long time the concept of the collective unconscious remained an intriguing theory without much proof. No one disputed that human nature has a dark side, but was Jung's explanation actually useful or was it just a brilliant intellectual invention? Only recently have bits and pieces of proof been gathered, and, if anything, they deepen the mystery. For example, it has been known for decades that when a person becomes lonely and isolated, as often happens to widows in old age, the risk of disease and death rises compared to that for people who have strong social connections. A happy marriage makes you healthy. At first this finding was hard to accept, because medical researchers saw no link between a mental state and the body. How could the heart or a precancerous cell somewhere in the body know how a person feels? It took the discovery of so-called messenger molecules to show that the brain translates every emotion into a chemical equivalent. As messenger molecules stream through the blood, circulating to hundreds of billions of cells, unhappiness or happiness gets transmitted to the heart, liver, intestines, and kidneys.

Suddenly mind-body medicine had a "real" basis, because nothing is more real than chemicals. But Jung was proposing that unhappiness or happiness could be shared by whole groups of people. Why does mass violence break out in Iraq or Rwanda? We can find explanations in long-standing tribal feuds and sectarian rifts. Are these stored in the collective unconscious, or do generations of parents tell their children to keep these ancestral grudges alive? It does no good to shake our heads and mutter about uncivilized, barbaric behavior. The greatest bloodbaths in history occurred during the two world wars. Millions of civilized soldiers marched into the jaws of death, men who wrote poetry, played the piano, knew Greek and Latin. Afterward, Europe looked back and called this slaughter insane, but eminently sane people ran the war and died in it, and when conscientious objectors protested, they were jailed or punished by being sent to the front lines as medics, a tragic irony that killed many of the people who hated war the most and wanted to prevent it.

The unconscious has a goal, which is to keep us unconscious. Sometimes knowledge peeks out anyway. In a famous social experiment at Stanford, psychologists replicated prison conditions to try to understand how guards treat prisoners. Undergraduates were divided into two groups, convicts and guards, and told to role-play any way they wanted. The psychologists in charge expected to be able to see marked changes in the behavior of each group, and yet the experiment had to be cut off in a matter of days. The students playing the part of guards began to severely mistreat the prisoners, to the point where humiliation and sexually charged abuse appeared. This stunning misfire gave rise to the theory of "good apples in bad barrels."

The old way of thinking had told psychologists that a bad apple can force a group to misbehave. Common sense says that a gang leader can induce his passive followers to commit crimes; college hazing goes too far because a small core of bad apples puts peer pressure on others. Yet the Stanford prison experiment told the opposite story. All the participants were good kids studying at a prestige university. Their misbehavior didn't occur because they were bad apples, but because they were in bad conditions that allowed dark forces to emerge. What the psychologists were seeing was nothing less than an incubator for the shadow, and the conditions that give rise to group violence were catalogued.

The shadow can emerge when there is complete anonymity, as often happens when, instead of being individuals, people become faces in a crowd. This loss of individuality increases if there are no consequences of one's bad actions. The absence of law and order amplifies the effect, as does being given permission to behave beyond normal morality. If authority figures are present to actively incite bad behavior and promise a lack of punishment, the shadow surfaces all the more easily. We don't have to make the barrel even worse by adding poverty, illiteracy, and old tribal ties, but they obviously taint conditions even more. So does any kind of "us versus them" thinking.

When I say that the shadow can emerge, I mean any kind of mass pathology can appear. The Stanford prison experiment resurfaced to explain the abuses at Abu Ghraib prison during the Iraq war. But if we realized that ghettos are also examples of "bad barrels" in which there are "good apples," we wouldn't resort to thinking of the underclass as morally inferior, or worse. The destruction of the ecosystem is a form of violence against the planet, yet it too involves good people doing very bad things because they have been given permission to and they face no punishment (except for the long-term harm that we all face, which can be ignored, denied, or put off until tomorrow). When people wake up from their misbehavior, they seem dazed and confused. The violence they perpetrated seems like a dream, even though they actively participated in horrors like war and genocide. The shadow traps us, therefore, in two ways. It keeps us unconscious and then erupts with incredible power whenever it wants to.

You may say, "What does this have to do with me?" Most of us haven't participated in an outbreak of the shadow like what occurred at Abu Ghraib. Instead of empathizing with the soldiers who abused their charges, we look for scapegoats to punish, because the bad-apple explanation is easier to live with. Yet when you do something as innocent as drive your car, you are putting nineteen pounds of carbon dioxide into the air, a greenhouse gas that is imperiling the planet. As a society we could rectify this bad behavior in a few years, once we put our minds to it. The solutions, from cleaner cars to mass transportation to alternative fuels, already exist. Why don't we exploit them fully? Because remaining unconscious is easier.

Skeptics have a right to point out that all of this still doesn't prove that there is a collective unconscious. Where is the evidence that members of a society are invisibly linked, without words or peer pressure binding them? A new field of sociology is studying "social contagion," a deeply mysterious phenomenon that could change everything we think about our behavior. We all experience how fads and trends work. Out of the blue, everybody seems to be doing something new, whether it's texting, fleeing MySpace for Twitter, or playing a new video game. Fads are contagious behavior. You catch them from other people. Yet no one knows how behavior goes viral. What makes a group of people all decide to act the same way?

This becomes a crucial medical question if you want a group to stop doing something harmful—if you want to persuade young people not to smoke, for example, or the general population to stop getting obese. The most advanced work on this question has come from two researchers at Harvard, Nicholas Christakis and James Fowler, whose new book, *Connected*, was previewed in a recent *New York Times* Sunday magazine article. Christakis and Fowler analyzed data from the nation's biggest heart study, which has followed three generations of citizens in Framingham, Massachusetts. They looked into the behavior of over five thousand people who were mapped according to fifty-one thousand social connections with family, friends, and coworkers.

Their first discovery was that when one person gained weight, started smoking, or got sick, close family members and friends were around 50 percent more likely to behave the same way. This reinforces a social-science principle that is decades old: behavior runs in groups. We have all experienced it as peer pressure or by observing behavioral traits that seem to "run in families." The reverse is also true. If you run with a healthy crowd, you are more likely to adopt healthy behavior yourself. Not just health is involved; almost any behavior can be contagious. In a dorm at college, if you happen to room with someone with good study habits and high grades, your grades are likely to improve by association.

But the second finding from Christakis and Fowler was far more mysterious. They found that social connections can skip a link. If person A is obese and knows person B, who isn't, a friend of person B is still 20 percent more likely to be obese, and a friend of that friend is 10 percent more likely. This "three degrees of connection" holds good for all kinds of behavior. A friend of a friend can make you prone to smoking, unhappiness, or loneliness. The statistics are there to prove it, even though you have never met this friend of a friend.

The findings of Christakis and Fowler suggest invisible connectors that run through a whole society. If their research holds up, think about the implications. The notion of a collective unconscious was posed almost a century ago by Jung. Did Jung hit on invisible connectors long before data came along to support them? That's really a side question to the main one: What kind of connections can exist invisibly, without people talking to each other, watching each other's behavior, or even knowing about each other's existence?

These are complex issues, and I'm giving only a hint of how mysterious they are. But the new research on social contagion is exciting, because it supports the notion that there is actually one mind that coordinates not just how people catch on to fads or decide to imitate each other, not just how distant brain cells know what other brain cells are doing, but far-flung phenomena like how twins separated by thousands of miles suddenly know what's happening to each other. These invisible connectors are bringing the collective unconscious into many, many areas of life. Social contagion is making news because we all like to rely on data, but the possibility that we all participate in one mind challenges religion, philosophy, and the meaning of life itself.

The shadow, then, is a shared project. Anyone can have a hand in building it. All you need is the ability to remain unconscious. Countless fear-mongers believe they are doing good. Every defender of the homeland expects to be honored and praised. Tribes warring against other tribes deeply believe that they must struggle in order to survive. We resist our shadow and deny its existence because of past indoctrination and the hypnosis of social conditioning. Childhood experiences cause unending later reminders that "this is good, this is bad; this is divine, this is diabolical." Such indoctrination is the way all societies are structured. What we overlook is that we are creating a shared self at the same time. If children were taught to become aware of their shadow, sharing even dark feelings, forgiving themselves for not being "good" all the time, learning how to release shadow impulses through healthy outlets, then there would be much less damage to society and the ecosystem.

Creators of the Shadow

Even if you haven't paid a moment's attention to Freud or Jung, you have inherited a different self because of them. They made it impossible to think about human nature as something other than a deep mystery. Like the tip of an iceberg, only a fraction of who you are is visible in the physical world. Unseen and often ignored, the human soul is a place of ambiguity, of contradiction and paradox. And that's as it should be, because all experience in life, which is the manifestation of the soul, is the result of contrast. You have no experience in the absence of contrast: light and shadow; pleasure and pain; up and down; backward and forward; hot and cold. If you didn't have these divisions, there would be no manifestation. Consciousness would be one vast flat field, like a desert. You would be aware of everything, but nothing in particular.

In order to have manifestation, you need opposing energies. That is why explicit enemies are also implicit allies. For example, Osama bin Laden and George Bush cocreated each other. On the surface they were enemies, but underneath they were allies. It's a general principle. You need your enemies to be who you are. Jung had the courage to see that each of us needs a dark side to be who we are. In fact, the collective unconscious is how the human race evolved, by passing on every new discovery in invisible form. These are primarily discoveries about the self.

It's a basic fact of physical anthropology that in *Homo sapiens* a massive part of the brain, the cortex, is devoted to higher functions. The cortex allows us to reason; it gave rise to love and compassion. Religion was born in the cortex, along with our concepts of heaven and hell. Without the higher brain, we would never have developed reading and writing, mathematics and art.

What a shock, then, to dig up the remains of Neanderthals, only to find that not only did that species have a huge cortex, but it was slightly bigger than ours. Yet Neanderthals roamed Europe hunting large animals for four hundred thousand years—twice as long as *Homo sapiens* has been around—using only one tool: a heavy spear with a stone point tied to it. Despite their huge cortex, Neanderthals never discovered a second tool. They didn't even progress to a lighter spear they could throw. Instead, they used their heavy spears to attack their prey, such as woolly mammoths and giant cave lions, at close quarters, thrusting the stone point into the animal's side. As a result, almost every male Neanderthal skeleton exhibits multiple fractures. Those big animals fought back, and yet for almost half a million years the Neanderthal brain couldn't figure out that it would be much safer to make lighter weapons that could be thrown from a distance.

The evolution of human beings depended not on the physical brain, but on the mind that used it. In the domain of the unconscious, learning was taking place, silently and out of sight. *Homo sapiens* was able to use the brain for much more complex things than any of its ancestors. Once the mind figured out how to make better weapons, life became easier. Farming replaced hunting and gathering. As life became more complicated, language arose so that people could exchange ideas.

In other words, Jung hit upon a secret place where all the action was. The collective unconscious is the mind's library, a storehouse of all past experience that we, in the present moment, can draw upon. The question "Who am I" never has a fixed answer. The self is fluid and constantly changing, meaning your own self and the self you share with everyone else. Studies have shown, for example, that the brains of people who have mastered computer skills and video games have new neural pathways unknown in the brains of people who are "digitally naïve," as the saying goes.

If we want to find the true self, we must dive into the shadow world and its constant flux. This has seemed like a dangerous quest, one that would cause all but the most heroic to turn pale. At the beginning of his famous film *Hamlet*, Laurence Olivier placed these words: "This is the story of a man who couldn't make up his mind." Hamlet has proof that his uncle killed his father in order to gain the crown of Denmark. He has every reason to seek revenge, and yet he can't. The perilous journey into the shadow, where killing and revenge are normal, threatens Hamlet's very existence, his nobility and civilized breeding. Even so, the prince does accept the perilous journey, and it leads him into disgust, self-loathing, the loss of love, and thoughts of suicide—typical reactions when you face the monsters of the deep. When he himself is finally murdered, Hamlet accepts his fate with relief and unearthly calm. The words at the beginning of Olivier's film should have been: "This is the story of a man afraid of his own shadow."

It's important, therefore, to realize that the shadow is a human creation. It was forged in the collective unconscious. Hating an enemy (yesterday it was Communists; today it's terrorists) isn't the fault of human nature. You and I inherited the feeling of enmity. It comes from the shadow, whose contents are of human construction. Specifically, the shadow sets up the model of "them," people who are alien from "us." "They" want to hurt us and take away what we value. Unlike us, they aren't fully human. We have a right to fight them, even destroy them. This invisible model, which shapes the minds of many people rather than one, which survives generation after generation to undermine rational thought, is what the shadow archetype is all about.

Human beings have consciously created vast civilizations as settings for our own evolution, yet at the unconscious level we have been amassing a history that goes far beyond the experience of any single person or epoch. What you call "me" is actually "us" to a far greater degree than you know.

The evidence can be found in your body. The immune system is a collective project. Under your breastbone lies a gland, the thymus, which produces the antibodies you need to resist infection from invading germs and viruses. When you are born, your thymus gland is undeveloped. You depend for the first year of life on immunity from your mother's body. But the thymus begins to grow and mature until it reaches maximum size and function at age twelve, after which it shrinks. During its period of growth, the thymus gives you antibodies for the diseases that were encountered by the entire human race.

You do not have to be infected by every disease; the inheritance of immunity is collective—and at the same time we keep adding to the storehouse as we confront new diseases.

This example shows that you don't have a separate physical body. Your body participates in a collective project, a process that never ends. I could have picked other examples, such as the evolution of the brain, but they all come down to DNA. Your genes record the history of human development on the physical level. Even though genetics hasn't revealed all the secrets of the genome, I think the next leap won't be physical—it will take place at the level of the soul. And the first task, once we arrive there, is to renew the soul itself. The era of the shadow can come to an end once we choose unity over separation. The fate of the divided self is in our hands.

The Process Continues

Where did the shadow come from? The impulse for separation created the contrast—and the war—between light and dark. When separation goes pathological, it manifests as the shadow's anger, fear, envy, and hostility. So the human soul feels simultaneously divine and diabolical, sacred and profane, saint and sinner. In Eastern wisdom traditions we have a saying that the sinner and the saint are merely exchanging notes. The sinner has a future and the saint has a past in which their roles are reversed. Forbidden lust and unconditional love are two sides of the same coin. You can't have a coin without a head and a tail, or an electrical current without a positive and a negative terminal.

Like electricity, life has no juice unless one pole sends a current to the other. Once you understand this, the first thing you realize is that to have a shadow is normal. The shadow is the separation impulse. But the divine impulse is the impulse that seeks unity. The choice to create a shadow has proved irresistible. It gave us the self we see as human, a familiar "I" who can be both good and bad. There is no real mystery there. The truly mysterious self enters when we ask if the power of self-creation can be used for something new: unity in place of division.

Separation has been a fascinating trip. The ego took human beings on a wild ride through bliss and tragedy. Our soul, this place of contradiction, paradox, and ambiguity, has constantly struggled between the two impulses, divine and diabolical. We see little reason to give up one for the other. We secretly love our bad boys and bad girls. Calling someone "devil may care" is a grudging compliment.

Yet from another perspective we have been wandering in the fog of illusion. Instead of exercising our power to create any self we want, we have passively inherited a split self, with all the misery and conflict it brings with it. Once you decide that "I, me, and mine" defines who you are, the perils of separation are inescapable. You can't have God without the Devil.

What is the Devil? It's the mythical shadow, the fallen angel, but it was born divine. In fact, another way of interpreting the word "devil" is as "the divine not feeling well." There's a shocking conclusion hidden in this: you can't have a universe if you don't have darkness contending with the light. Contrast doesn't sound exciting, but once it exploded into the visible universe, the result was incredibly dramatic: a living hologram of good and evil. There isn't an atom or subatomic particle in the cosmos that hasn't been enlisted into the drama of opposites, starting with electrical charges and ascending to the battle between Satan and God.

The visible universe gave us the scenic backdrop for our evolution; the invisible domain gave us the soul. The two go hand in hand. In fact, they are one. Any change you make at the level of the soul also creates a change in the outer world, which is the mirror of the soul. You are not stuck with inheriting the same old drama in which a fallen, sinful soul struggles to reach the light—and may or may not succeed. That spiritual drama underpins the ego's wild ride. It turns the whole world into a playground for good and evil, and all that goes with it: sin and redemption, temptation and righteousness. The notion of creating a new soul—and a new story line to go with it—is both strange and exciting.

The impulse for separation gave us the reality we know. What impulse will give us a new reality? Call it the holographic impulse. The holographic impulse bypasses details and aims for wholeness. It creates three-dimensional settings in which inner and outer fuse into one. Most people have seen a hologram created by using laser light. By taking no more than the fragment of a photo or an object, the laser can re-create the entire object or photo, as if by magic. Instead of a fragment, wholeness pops into view. In the same way, even though you are preoccupied by the fragments of everyday life—errands, cooking, work, leisure, likes and dislikes, a hundred small choices between A and B—your mind has actually projected a hologram for you to inhabit. You live inside a wholeness. The holographic impulse cannot be switched off or destroyed. Even though you may look around and dislike much of what you see in your personal world, feeling trapped by other people and difficult situations, you retain the power to create a totally new hologram. A new hologram implies a new self. Neither can be achieved one piece at a time. It's easier to create wholeness, in fact, than to change your reality one fragment at a time.

To have holistic change, you must operate from the level of holistic creation. There's a fascinating exercise that gives a hint at how this might work. Close your eyes and imagine a vivid visual experience, such as a tropical sunset or a high alpine peak. The image itself can be anything, so long as you can envision it with color and depth. Now imagine a taste you love, such as rich chocolate or coffee. Go into that sensation deeply until you actually taste it. Move on to a sound you love, such as your favorite music, then a delightful texture, like velvet, and finally an intoxicating smell, such as a damask rose or lily.

Having imagined these vivid experiences in all the five senses, open your eyes. You will be startled at what you see. The ordinary world is vividly alive. Colors are brighter. A vibrancy hangs in the air. This startling change is reported by everyone, and it demonstrates that even slightly heightening your inner world causes the outer world to automatically follow suit. What we have here is a clue to one of the deepest of spiritual secrets, the power to alter reality all at once. Such power isn't available on the surface of life, which is why people feel tossed about by their external circumstances. You must find the level of the soul, where the holographic impulse can create anything.

Jung called it the collective *unconscious* rather than the collective *conscious* for this very reason. Human beings have collectively created the world without knowing that it was happening. Here are the main ingredients we used. Notice how they spiral deeper and deeper from the first, which seems rather harmless, to the last, which is highly self-destructive:

Secrecy: We learned not to reveal our basic drives and desires.

Guilt and shame: Once the basic drives and desires were hidden, they felt bad.

Judgment: Anything that felt bad became wrong.

Blame: We wanted to know who was responsible for the pain we felt.

Projection: A convenient scapegoat was manufactured, either a hated enemy or an invisible demonic force.

Separation: We did everything we could to push this demonic force outside ourselves. Enemies were "the other," who had to be guarded against and fought with.

Struggle: Projection couldn't make the pain go away permanently, so a constant state of inner-versus-outer warfare ensued.

As you can see, the shadow is still being fueled, because we are masters at manipulating these ingredients. We are addicted to them, in fact, even though the result is war, violence, crime, and endless struggle, not to mention the stifling effect of believing in cosmic evil as a presence in the world. The solution is to uncreate the shadow. It's not Frankenstein's monster, a horror that has grown more powerful than its creator. The shadow is a region of the psyche. Nothing exists in it that is beyond our power to dissolve. Instead of allowing the shadow to victimize us, we must seize the control switch and reclaim our true function as creators.

THE WAY OUT

Let me summarize the argument up to now in three sentences. *Duality is where you are. The shadow has surrounded you with a fog of illusion. Your split self is the first and most damaging illusion.* Now let's engage the problem personally, by seeing if the diagnosis actually fits.

The shadow may be hard for you to see when you look around on this or any other day. For most of us, everyday life isn't pathological. Even though experts tell us that domestic and sexual abuse is far more widespread than we want to admit, even though depression and anxiety disorders continue to rise at an alarming rate, ordinary people find it easy to deny the darker side of human nature. So it's important to know that the shadow isn't a bogeyman. Anything that keeps you unconscious is the result of the shadow, because the shadow is the hiding place of pain and stress. Mass outbreaks of violence occur when social stress cannot be suppressed any longer. Domestic violence occurs when personal stress cannot be contained. The price of remaining unconscious is very high.

Let's make this more personal. The forces that have been employed over the ages to create the collective shadow are being used by you today. The unconscious may seem like an amorphous sea, a dark chaos of impulses, drives, secrets, and taboos all jumbled together. But we can separate out the various strands and make sense of them. Consider the following chart:

"Me and My Shadow"

Like everything in life, creating the shadow is a process. No one sets out to increase the power of the shadow, yet we all do. The shadow increases whenever you resort to the following:

Keeping secrets from yourself and others. A secretive life gives the shadow material to build upon. Forms of secrecy are denial, deliberate deception, fear of exposing who you are, and conditioning by a dysfunctional family.

Harboring guilt and shame. Everyone is fallible; no one is perfect. But if you feel ashamed of your mistakes and guilty about your imperfections, the shadow gains power.

Making yourself and others wrong. If you can't find a way to release your guilt and shame, it's all too easy to decide that you—or others—deserve them. Judgment is guilt wearing a moral mask to disguise its pain.

Needing someone to blame. Once you decide that your inner pain is a moral issue, you will have no trouble blaming someone else you feel is inferior to you in some way.

Ignoring your own weaknesses while criticizing those around you. This is the process of projection, which many don't see or understand very well. But whenever you try to explain a

situation as the act of God or the Devil, you are projecting. The same goes for identifying "them," the bad people
who cause all the problems. If you believe the problem is
with "them," you have projected your own fear instead of
taking responsibility for it.

Separating yourself from others. If you reach the point where
you feel that the world is divided into "them" and "us,"
you will naturally identify your side as the good one and
choose it. This isolation increases a sense of fear and sus-
picion, which the shadow thrives on.

Struggling to keep evil at bay. At the bottom of the cycle, people
are convinced that evil lurks everywhere. What has really
happened is that the creators of illusion are being fooled
by their own creation. Everything has come together to
give the shadow enormous power.

We've taken the first step in removing the shadow's power by exposing the process that fuels it. There's a downward spiral. It begins
by thinking you have to keep secrets, and then those secrets, instead
of remaining quietly hidden, become the source of shame and guilt.
Self-judgment enters. This is too painful to live with, so you search
for someone outside yourself to blame. The spiral leads eventually to
isolation and denial. By the time you find yourself struggling with sin
and evil, you have long ago lost sight of the basic fact that would save
you, which isn't redemption from the Devil. The basic fact is that
you entered this whole process willingly by making simple choices.
Therefore to escape you only need to make the opposite choices.

I've divided those choices into four categories with steps to take
toward making them:

I. Stop projecting.

2. Detach and let go.

3. Give up self-judgment.

4. Rebuild your emotional body.

The basic life choices are available to anyone. We make the opposite choices all the time. The shadow has persuaded us to blame others rather than take responsibility. It tells us that we are unworthy of love and respect. It promotes anger and fear as natural reactions to life. All of us are entangled in these disastrous choices. They stifle our lives and remove all joy. So nothing is more urgent than to turn the process around, and the sooner the better.

Step I: Stop Projecting

The shadow, according to Jung, tells us to ignore our own weaknesses and project them on others. To avoid feeling that we're not good enough, we see others around us as not good enough. Countless examples come to mind. Some are trivial, while others are a matter of life and death. The latest movie starlet is criticized for losing too much weight while a whole nation becomes more obese. Antiwar movements are denounced as unpatriotic, while everyone is paying taxes to kill citizens of a country that has never done America any harm. Everyone uses projection as a defense to avoid looking inward.

Realize that this is an unconscious defense. The template of projection is the following statement: "I can't admit what I feel, so I'll imagine that you feel it." Thus, if you can't feel your own anger, you label a group in society as violent and to be feared. If you unconsciously have sexual feelings you consider taboo, such as attraction to someone of the same gender or thoughts of infidelity, you think that others are directing those feelings toward you.

Projection is very effective. A false state of self-acceptance is created based on "I'm okay, but you aren't." Yet true self-acceptance extends to other people; when you are okay with yourself, there's no reason to label anyone as not okay.

Are You Projecting?

Here are the typical forms that projection can take:

Superiority: "I know that I'm better than you. You should see this and acknowledge it."

Injustice: "It's unfair that these bad things are happening to me," or "I don't deserve this."

Arrogance: "I'm too proud to bother with you. Your very presence irritates me."

Defensiveness: "You're attacking me, so I'm not listening to you."

Blame: "I didn't do anything. It's all your fault."

Idealizing others: "My father was like a god when I was little," "My mother was the best in the world," or "The man I marry will be my hero."

Prejudice: "He's one of them, and you know what they're like," or "Be careful. Their kind is dangerous."

Jealousy: "You're thinking of betraying me. I can see it."

Paranoia: "They're out to get me," or "I see the conspiracy no one else sees."

Whenever any of these attitudes appear, there is an unconscious feeling hidden in the shadow that you cannot face. Here are some typical examples:

Superiority disguises the feeling that you are a failure or that others would reject you if they knew who you really are.

Injustice disguises the feeling of sinfulness or the sense that you are always to blame.

Arrogance disguises bottled-up anger, and beneath that lies deep-seated pain.

Defensiveness disguises the feeling that you are unworthy and weak. Unless you defend yourself from others, you will start attacking yourself.

Blame disguises the feeling that you are at fault and should be ashamed of yourself.

Idealizing others disguises the feeling that you are a weak, helpless child who needs protection and taking care of.

Prejudice disguises the feeling that you are inferior and deserve to be rejected.

Jealousy disguises your own impulse to stray or a sense of sexual inadequacy.

Paranoia disguises deep-seated, overwhelming anxiety.

As you can see, projection is far more subtle than anyone imagines. Yet it is the open gate to the shadow. It is a painful gate, though, since what you see as faults in others masks what you feel about yourself. It would be ideal if we could stop blaming and judging all at once. In reality, undoing the shadow is always a process. To stop projecting you must see what you're doing, contact the feeling that is hidden beneath the surface, and make peace with that feeling.

See what you're doing: Is it easy to recognize when you're projecting? One clue is negativity—projection is never neutral. It manifests as negative energy because what it's disguising is negative. This turns out to be a help. You know when you're feeling angry or anxious. Those are shadow feelings. But when you are aiming your anger at someone or something or seeing reasons everywhere to be afraid (negativity is present), you have a clear example of projection. I hope you can see the difference between feelings and projecting those feelings; feeling angry is useful, while aiming anger in the form of blame isn't. Society wants you to keep blaming, because "us versus them" thinking is a way—a very bad way—to hold society together. Hence the small voice inside your head that wants to get "them"—the terrorists, the godless Communists, the drug dealers, criminals, or child abusers. The list is endless. Instead of buying into all the reasons for blaming "them" and judging all their faults (reasons that can be valid), take a different path. Look at yourself and what the blame game says about you.

One time the noted Indian spiritual teacher J. Krishnamurti was giving a talk, and someone in the audience stood up to ask a question. "I want peace in the world. I abhor war. What can I do to bring about peace?"

"Stop being the cause of war," Krishnamurti replied.

The questioner was taken aback. "I am not in favor of war. I only want peace."

Krishnamurti shook his head. "Inside you is the cause of every war. It is your violence, hidden and denied, that leads to wars of every kind, whether it is war inside your home, against others in society, or between nations."

His reply makes us uncomfortable, but I think it's true, because the Vedic *rishis* (seers) proclaimed, "You are not in the world. The world is in you." If that is so, then the violence of the world is in each of us. Before the concept of the shadow emerged, such a statement sounded mystical. But once you see that you are participating in a shared self, you can also see that every impulse of anger, fear, resentment, and aggression leads directly from you to the collective unconscious and back again.

I realize that catching yourself every time you project your own hidden negativity isn't always easy. Denial is powerful. The shadow is secretive. When you idealize somebody else, a hero you hold up to the light and call perfect, it's hard to see any underlying negativity. But there is, because this fantasy of perfection in someone else hides a deep sense of inferiority in yourself. But if you go back to the chart about projection and consult it often, you will find it easier to catch yourself using this defense.

Contact your hidden feelings: The minute you see that you are projecting a hidden feeling is the moment you need to contact it. Don't delay. The door of opportunity closes very quickly. But before it does, there's a gap. Just before you erect your defense, you actually feel the thing you don't want to feel.

Here's an example given to me by a young man. He was very poor in graduate school, but had prosperous friends who used to invite him to dinner. One night sitting around the table, he thought of a curious anecdote.

"Remember when we were in London last summer?" he said, turning to his host. "You and your wife started arguing right there on the sidewalk. You both raised your voices, while I just stood there. You were so busy screaming, you didn't notice that a van had pulled up behind you. On the side of the van were the words 'Blue Tantrum.' I guess that's an example of synchronicity or something."

The other guests nodded and murmured, and the conversation moved on. But afterward the hostess took the young man aside. "Why did you want to humiliate us like that?" she asked angrily.

"I wasn't humiliating you," he protested. "I was telling a story that I thought was interesting."

"Go back," the hostess said. "Put yourself in the moment when you decided to tell the story. What did you feel?"

The young man shrugged. "Nothing. The story just came to me."

She shook her head. "No, at that moment you had a malicious impulse. Not just any story came to mind. One that embarrassed us did."

Not many people have the nerve, or the acumen, to analyze a fleeting moment in this way. It's to the young man's credit that the confrontation worked. He told me, "I didn't automatically defend myself. I went back, and she was right. I had felt jealous at that moment. Here was a table of food and wine I couldn't afford to buy. At a certain level, it was humiliating to be there and know I couldn't reciprocate." Which is why, to hide his own humiliation, he turned the situation around and told a story in which someone else was humiliated.

In this little example we see the traits you need if you want to feel what is hidden inside: alertness, willingness, openness, honesty, and courage. Or to put it another way, if you don't stop yourself and ask, "What am I really feeling right now?" you are turning your back on alertness, willingness, openness, honesty, and courage. You are letting the shadow win.

Make peace with your feelings: Once you can feel what's really there, you have a choice. Several choices, actually. You can push the feeling back down. You can blame yourself for not being a good person. You can attack the feeling, lament it, or apologize for it. None of these choices are productive. They play into the shadow's hands by reinforcing the unwanted feeling and making it even more unwanted.

It sounds strange, but feelings have feelings. Being part of you, they know when they are unwanted. Fear cooperates by hiding; anger cooperates by pretending it doesn't exist. That's more than half the problem. How can you heal an unwanted feeling when it's trying not to cooperate? You can't. Until you make peace with negative feelings, they will persist. The way to deal with negativity is to acknowledge it. Nothing more is needed. No dramatic confrontation, no catharsis. Feel the feeling, whether it's anger, fear, envy, aggression, or anything else, and say, "I see you. You belong to me." You don't have to feel fine about your unwanted feeling. This is a process. Anger and fear will return; so will any deeply hidden emotion. When one does, acknowledge it. As time goes on, the message will get through. Your unwanted feelings will start to feel less unwanted.

When that happens, you will begin to hear their story. Packaged inside every feeling is a tale: "I am this way for a reason." Be open to the story that comes out, no matter what it is. Every past trauma you have ever experienced, from a car accident to rejection in love, from losing a job to failing in school, has deposited its remains in the shadow. You have been accumulating what some psychologists call "emotional debt to the past." To pay back this debt, you listen to the story that lies behind it. Let's say the story is "I never got over not making the baseball team" or "I feel guilty that I stole money from Mom's purse." Most stories are rooted in childhood, because childhood is the learning ground for guilt, shame, resentment, inferiority, and all of the most primal negativity we carry around with us.

Having heard the story, be accepting. Tell yourself that you had a valid reason for holding on to negativity. You had no choice, because it was secretly deposited and then remained hidden. Therefore, you did nothing wrong. Your old feelings stuck around to protect you from having the same wound repeated. Make peace with this now, and you have turned a negative into a positive. Fear wasn't holding on to hurt you; it thought you needed to be on guard in case of another hurt—another girl or guy rejects you, another parent scolds you, another boss fires you. But those things aren't going to happen again, certainly not in the very same way.

The last thing you want to do is to recycle these old emotions. That's very tempting, of course. Caught in a frustrating situation, we're all tempted to reach into our bag of emotions and haul out anger. At tense moments we reach in and pull out anxiety. However, if you keep recycling emotions from the past, you will only wind up reinforcing the past.

None of us need to protect ourselves from a childhood that is long past. Even if similar situations occur—not that anyone can predict them—all of us are overprotected already. We don't store one reason to be afraid, but dozens and dozens, and just so we don't forget them, we participate in collective fear about enemies, crime, natural disasters, and so forth. It won't do you any harm to make peace with as much fear, anger, and aggression as you can. The psyche will still remember what it needs to.

Having learned how to deal with projection, you can ask the next question. Why do you need to defend yourself at all? This becomes a key issue, because it calls into question the main reason the shadow exists.

Step 2: Detach and Let Go

Why is it hard to let go of negative emotions? There's more than one reason. First, negative emotions are the tip of the iceberg, so every time you get angry or anxious, for example, there is much more of those feelings stored in the shadow. Second, negativity is sticky. It holds on to us just as much as we hold on to it. This stickiness is a survival mechanism. Feelings think they have a right to exist. Like you, your emotions justify their existence. They offer reasons; they build a convincing story. Despite all these things, however, you can let go of negativity once you know how.

The process begins by acknowledging your feelings, however unwanted, and bringing them to the surface. We've covered that step. Now you need to detach yourself from the negativity. There's a balancing act here, because you want to take responsibility ("This is mine") without going overboard and identifying with your negativity ("This is me"). Negativity isn't you once you know your true self, which is beyond the shadow. So consider any negative reaction as though it were like an allergy or the flu, something that changes your situation for the moment only. An allergy is yours, but it isn't you.

The flu brings misery, but that doesn't mean you are doomed to be a miserable person.

When you find ways to undo the stickiness of negativity, you will become more detached. The following statements work toward detachment:

"I can get through this. It won't last forever."

"I've felt this way before. I can deal with it."

"I won't feel better unloading on someone else."

"No one ever wins the blame game."

"Acting out leads to regret and guilt."

"I can be patient. Let's see if I cool down in a while."

"I'm not alone. I can call someone to help me through this bad patch."

"I am much more than my feelings."

"Moods come and go, even the worst moods."

"I know how to center myself."

If you can make any of these statements true, then you are adding to your coping skills. How do you make them true? By wanting them to be. You must intend to be detached, centered, patient, and self-aware. If you have that intention, automatically you are aligning with detachment. The opposite is to be so attached that you increase the stickiness of negativity. That occurs when you have the following kinds of thoughts:

"I feel horrible. I don't deserve this. Why me?"

"Somebody's going to pay. I didn't bring this on myself."

"Who can I unload this on?"

"This is making me crazy."

"Nobody can help me."

"How can I distract myself until this feeling goes away?"

"I need my drug of choice to get through this."

"When I'm feeling this bad, everybody better look out."

"I want to be rescued."

"Somebody has it in for me."

"This has to be settled right now."

"I can't help how I feel. It's just how I'm wired."

I realize that "detachment" is a term that people in the West identify with Eastern fatalism or indifference. So make this the first concept you reframe in a positive way. Detachment doesn't show indifference. It shows that you really don't want negativity to stick to you.

Step 3: Give Up Self-Judgment

You get the emotions you think you deserve. Yet many times these aren't the emotions you want. Far from it. Everyone is in the position of juggling "bad" feelings with "good" ones, which comes down to self-judgment. Wrapped up in the "bad" feelings—anger, fear, envy, hostility, victimization, self-pity, and aggression—is a self-image that needs these negative emotions. No two people use them exactly alike. We build up our identities in unique ways. Some people use fear to motivate themselves to overcome challenges; others use it to feel dependent and victimized. Some deploy anger to control anyone in their vicinity; others are afraid of anger and never show it. Yet your sense of self, and therefore your self-worth, are tied up in every feeling you have.

Every emotion is valid in some way or another. But when you add the ingredient of self-judgment, any emotion can be damaging. Love has destroyed lives when it was misplaced, warped, or rejected. "I was only trying to help" sounds like a positive statement born of caring, but how often does it mask unwelcome intrusion? You can shape a nonjudgmental self-image anytime you want. Countless people want to, and almost as many experts tell us how. But if your emotions have negative effects, you won't be able to create the self you want. It's very difficult to feel good about yourself if primal emotions like anger and fear are allowed to have their own way. So, what to do? If repression and suppression don't work, neither does letting negative emotions run free.

I place a high value on sympathy. If you can look at yourself and say, "It's all right. I understand," you are doing two things at once. You are taking the judgment out of your emotions, and you are giving yourself permission to be who you are. Sympathy is an emotion we tend to direct outward. We forget to grant it to ourselves. I was reminded of this by a striking encounter I had with a young woman who came up to ask me a question.

"I listen to people all the time," she said. "I was just wondering, can being sympathetic go too far?"

I asked her to describe what happens when she listens to people.

"It's strange," she said. "When I get up in the morning I listen to my family and sympathize. I've been that way since I was a child. At work people bring me their troubles, because they know I will be sympathetic. But recently even people on the street, perfect strangers, suddenly come up to me to tell me their troubles. I hear all kinds of stories."

"And you always take the time to offer sympathy?" I asked. She nodded.

"I don't think you're harming yourself," I said. She looked relieved. "In fact," I went on, "I think you are remarkable without realizing it. I'm grateful you exist."

This was unexpected, and she was embarrassed. Not many of us can say that our main problem is an excess of sympathy for others.

"But there are pitfalls," I told her. "Sympathy is a synonym for compassion. The word 'compassion' means to suffer with. That's where one must draw the line. Your sympathy will be ill-spent if it exhausts you. It must not overwhelm you or cause you to feel as bad as the one you sympathize with," I said.

When it's valid, compassion is as valuable for the one who gives it as for the one who receives it. Afterward, I thought about how this applies to the self. Inside each of us is a voice that sits in judgment. Call it a conscience or the superego, this voice doesn't come from an outside judge or parent. But it acts independent, evaluating the worth of who we are and what we're thinking. Let's say you get angry at someone unjustly and later feel guilty about flying off the handle. The judgmental voice in your head says, "You were wrong. You probably got yourself in trouble, and you deserve it." Perhaps these words are helpful in a certain way. But this judgmental voice is just you; therefore, in judging against you, it is actually judging against itself. There is no independent, objective judge inside. The voice that labels you as wrong or bad is a fictional character, and what you'll notice is that this character never sympathizes. To keep its power over you, it must intimidate you.

What would happen if you started to sympathize with yourself? The inner judge would begin to dissolve. In the case of this young woman, I sensed that she wasn't manipulating her sympathy selfishly, as people do when they say, "After seeing how badly off my friend is, I feel much better about myself." Instead, she was letting her sympathy flow by listening and opening a channel. We must do the same for ourselves. Even better if that channel leads to God. At its highest, compassion has a healing role to play. When you offer sympathy, the woes of another are heard and passed on to a higher level of awareness.

We're not talking about renouncing your conscience. But when conscience becomes punishing and makes you feel unworthy, it has gone too far. It's time to release the judgment that keeps you bound inside a narrow self-conception. In the realm of spirit or God—call it what you will—suffering can be healed. Through your sympathy, you open a channel to the healing powers. Aspire to be such a channel. It is one of life's greatest joys, and certainly the purest.

Step 4: Rebuild Your Emotional Body

As any negative emotion surfaces, you can replace it with something new. I call this rebuilding your emotional body. We all have a mental image of what a desirable physical body is like—trim, healthy, youthful, fresh, pleasing to look at. But we don't use those qualities with regard to our emotions, our "emotional body." The emotional body, like the physical body, must be properly nourished. It can grow tired and flabby when the same responses to the world are repeated over and over. It becomes diseased when exposed to toxins and unhealthy influences.

Every time you feel a negative emotion, your emotional body is expressing discomfort, soreness, fatigue, or pain. Pay attention to these symptoms just as you would to physical pain and discomfort. If you had a rock in your shoe, you wouldn't hesitate to remove it. Yet how long have you endured emotional rocks in your shoe? In many ways, our priorities should be reversed. Think of the time and money spent to avoid aging. We expend enormous effort and care to make sure that our bodies can be healthy and functional into advanced old age. Yet ironically, it's the emotional body that is immune to aging. There is no reason for emotions ever to grow old, because the source of freshness and renewal is always at hand. Your emotional body should remain energetic, alert, flexible, and pleasing to experience. I think a single phrase, "the lightness of being," covers all of these qualities.

Children naturally feel lightness in their being. They play and laugh; they forget traumas and bounce back quickly. Whatever they feel quickly comes to the surface. This carefree period may not last long. Observing a young child closely, you can see the beginning of tendencies that will lead to future suffering, as the shadow teaches its tactics of projection, blame, guilt, and all the rest. That's why rebuilding the emotional body is the best long-term strategy for everyone—your future depends on undoing your past. The key is to have a vision. Then you can implement your vision every day. There's no lack of detailed advice, in this book and from many other sources. But without a vision, even the best advice becomes haphazard and piecemeal.

A vision for rebuilding the emotional body includes at least some of the following points:

Becoming more whole

Learning to be resilient

Dispelling the demons of the past

Healing old wounds

Expecting the best and highest for yourself

Adopting realistic ideals

Giving of yourself

Being generous, especially with your spirit

Seeing through your fears

Learning self-acceptance

Communicating with God or your higher self

The most important single thing in rebuilding your emotional body is becoming more whole. Emotions can't be reshaped in isolation. They merge and blend with thoughts, actions, aspirations, wishes, and relationships. Every feeling you have invisibly moves outward into your environment, affecting the people around you and ultimately society and the world at large. Having worked with thousands of people over the years, I've come to see that without wholeness, all we can create is superficial change. Therefore, let's see if we can approach your life as one reality, a process that encompasses every thought and action you have ever had or will have.

This may sound rather overwhelming, but to escape the fog of illusion, the only way out is reality. In truth there is only one reality. You have no way of separating yourself from it. Nor would you wish to once you see the enormous advantage of living in wholeness. Your separate self, which has such a huge personal stake in the world, isn't who you really are. In fact, it may be a total illusion, which is what the Buddha said. The self you defend every day as your unique point of view is a convenient fiction that makes the ego feel good. What the ego doesn't realize, however, is that it would feel even better if it gave up its narrow, selfish stake in the world. When that happens, the true self can emerge. Then and only then is wholeness possible.

A NEW REALITY, A NEW POWER

Wholeness overcomes the shadow by absorbing it. Evil and wrongdoing are no longer isolated. Earlier I mentioned that damaging the ecosystem is an example of how misbehavior can be denied and swept under the carpet. But as attitudes change, we've discovered that the ecosystem is totally interconnected. Everyone's behavior affects everyone else. There is no part of the planet that can be isolated, as if immune to ecological harm done by other parts. Wholeness changes our entire perspective.

Now expand the word "ecosystem" to a broader context. Wholeness must expand to take account of the laws that control pollution, social battles over global warming, personal attitudes about recycling, and ultimately our very way of being happy. Can we continue to be happy with a way of life that is slowly destroying the natural world? Everything you can possibly think of is encompassed by the ecosystem. It is the web of relationships in which we all exist. If you understand the web of relationships as an invisible place where everything comes together, you begin to see wholeness where divisions once existed.

In the current debate over the environment, two paths lie open. We can continue to deny the problem or we can face it. The first path is a false solution, because it doesn't resolve the underlying fear and guilt of ecological destruction and future disasters. The second path eliminates fear and guilt the only way that proves viable: by solving the problem that leads to those emotions. The same holds true for the shadow. The problem calls for a holistic approach to solve it. Denial is a false solution.

If you acknowledge and embrace your shadow, it is actually nurturing, because the whole of life is nurturing—that is, life exists to sustain itself. When we get stuck in the drama of good versus evil, we impose our own limited perspective. After all, even when someone is committing a violent crime or going to war or victimizing someone else, the wrongdoer's cells and organs don't shut down. The body's allegiance is to life, no matter how confused and conflicted the mind becomes.

A New Worldview

The miracle plays of the Middle Ages, which were performed on feast days, took the grim seriousness of evil and turned it into a cosmic joke. The Devil is a comic character who engages in every kind of bad deed, tempting souls and bringing torment, yet the Devil fails to see that in the end God is more powerful. Satan himself will be redeemed. In the end, the joke is on him; no one is out of God's reach. In religious terms these miracle plays are saying that wholeness always overcomes separation. If you see the world in terms of good versus evil, you have missed the cosmic joke.

Whatever you think is wrong about yourself and too painful to confront can be seen a different way. Life—meaning your life and mine—transcends any win-or-lose orientation. Wholeness goes beyond simplistic cause-and-effect explanations. In the web of relationship, you function in a much larger context. Once you see yourself as part of the whole, a new understanding arises. There is no need to label yourself or anyone else as part of the good-versus-evil, right-versus-wrong drama. You can exchange judgment for the real experience of compassion, love, and forgiveness. That is the healing that comes with being whole.

But the holistic viewpoint also unleashes a deeper intuitive know-ingness—you see why things are the way they are. It's common to hear people say, "There's a reason for everything that happens," but usually, if asked what the reason is, they don't actually know. The mind keeps searching in vain for cause-and-effect explanations. This effort gets us into strange speculations: "I once cheated on my wife and now this bankruptcy is payback"; "I used to be full of anger, and now I have cancer"; "The community quit believing in God's com-mandments, and now a hurricane has leveled it." Even if you reject such dark connections, you probably still harbor superstitions along the same lines, because we all do. We weren't taught another way to explain the unseen workings of reality.

Let me suggest another way. What if everything that exists, visible or invisible, fits into a single scheme? In this scheme, the entire uni-verse is made of consciousness. The largest events, such as the birth and death of galaxies, are connected to the smallest, the interactions of subatomic particles. Everything is part of one consciousness, which earlier ages called the mind of God. We don't have to use religious terms. But like the traditional concept of God, consciousness is infinite, all-embracing, all-powerful, and all-knowing. It unfolds into myriad forms and shapes. Viewed through the five senses, some of these forms don't appear conscious. It sounds peculiar to say that a jellyfish pulsating in the Pacific Ocean, a rock on the side of Mt. Everest, and a raindrop falling in Brazil are conscious. But we're not talking about possessing a brain. A jellyfish, a rock, and a raindrop don't have thoughts and feelings (so far as we know—it's good to keep an open mind about the unknown). Therefore, we don't feel intimately connected to the "nonconscious" life around us.

When we stand apart from objects and lower creatures, as we call them, something huge is being missed. There are principles that embrace all things. Look at a cell in your body and an electron hurtling through the darkness of space, and at an invisible level some deep similarities emerge:

Every action is coordinated with every other action.

Information is shared by every part of the whole.

Communication is instantaneous.

Energy is reshaped into countless variations, yet never lost.

Evolution produces more intricate forms as time unfolds.

Consciousness expands as forms become more complex.

These are very abstract terms, I know, but ultimately there is no need for words at all. When you see yourself as separate, words seem to matter much more than being. After all, being is passive, something we take for granted, while words run our lives, fill our heads, bring people together, and drive them apart. Yet all these words couldn't exist without the silent intelligence inside every cell. The power that holds your body together, coordinating an infinite number of biological actions per second among hundreds of billions of cells, is more primal than thinking and using words.

Primal doesn't mean primitive, a mistake we make when we get too proud of human reason. The consciousness found everywhere is inexpressible; it far exceeds the human mind. If we list the things that come to us from a mysterious source, that we experience deeply without words, it's a wonder that anyone ever doubted the existence of the invisible world. Here's a short list:

Love

Creativity

The sense of being alive

Beauty

Inspiration

Intuition

Dreams

Visions

Yearning

Fulfillment

The sense of belonging

Awe, wonder

Ecstasy, bliss

The numinous, a sense of the divine

A life filled with all these invisible qualities would be nothing less than a new way of being. No one would willingly refuse wonder, creativity, love, and all the rest. Yet millions of people do. They experience bliss and fulfillment in small doses that quickly fade. They fail to get past the shadow, which guards the riches of the unconscious with sharp claws and fangs. I once heard a guru lament to his audience, "I show you the gates of heaven, and when a goblin springs up shouting 'Boo!' you run away."

Fear, anger, insecurity, anxiety, and the other aspects of the shadow feel like much more than "Boo!" If we are going to reach heaven's gates, the only self that can get us there is the one we have. That's the dilemma. How can a divided self ever attain wholeness? I'd like to propose that it can, but the way isn't what most seekers think it is. Krishnamurti, the most dry-eyed, even ruthless of Indian sages, said, "Freedom isn't the end of the path. It's the beginning. There is nowhere to go. Freedom is the first and the last thing on the path." He wasn't trying to mystify his followers. Krishnamurti's doctrine of the first and last freedom, as he dubbed it, was his way of saying that wholeness—the state of complete freedom—isn't about choosing this or that. It isn't about being good instead of bad, pure instead of impure. Wholeness has no divisions. It is everything. Therefore, it must be the beginning and the end at the same time. Our job is to turn this insight into a practical way of life.

What Is Wholeness Like?

The glory of human existence doesn't lie in all the things that make us unique. It lies in the fact that we can unite with cosmic intelligence; each of us can become a conscious part of the whole. When that happens, you gain a world that is barely suggested by the thoughts and feelings of everyday life. It's practical to live holistically, because with all of consciousness to draw upon, you will be much more creative and imaginative, much less judgmental. But for any of these benefits to come about, you have to experience what wholeness is really like. Let's go into that now.

Wholeness Wants to Heal You

Wholeness always tries to restore itself. Your body has a complete array of healing techniques. Wholeness and healing are intimately connected (the two words derive from the same root word in Sanskrit). What does the body do to restore wholeness?

It seeks balance.

Every cell communicates with every other.

No part is more important than the whole.

Rest and activity are harmonized.

In the midst of constant activity, there is a stable foundation (known as homeostasis).

Every cell adapts to change in the environment.

Stress is countered and brought under control (disease and discomfort are basically the result of stress).

In each case, the body is keeping itself whole. The healing system extends everywhere. Your heart, brain, and liver cells all perform different functions, but keeping alive and healthy is their common goal; therefore, wholeness is more important than any single activity. If you look at your body as a metaphor for your life, what does it mean?

You will value balance.

The separate aspects of your life will work toward a common purpose.

Every aspect of living will assume equal value.

Rest will find a normal rhythm with activity.

Your core self, which is calm and at peace, won't be disturbed in the midst of activity.

As your situation changes, you will adapt and remain resilient.

At the first signs that stress is throwing you out of your comfort zone, you will notice and respond.

You will value your well-being over any individual experience.

I've couched these points in general terms, but consider how differently two people would live if one chose wholeness and the other didn't.

Wholeness Is Always a Gain, Never a Loss

To be whole is to be fully healed. If that is true, then no matter how well you live your life, you are not fully healed until the split self has been transformed. There are many ways to achieve a good life, and countless people find reasons not to seek wholeness (one of the biggest reasons for this is that they have never been exposed to a vision of the higher self as it really exists). It's crucial to know that you won't stop being yourself if you seek transformation.

The world of contrasts is seductive and dramatic. Without contrast, would we be doomed to eternal sameness? The stronger the light, the greater the shadow. This isn't something created by humankind; it's the way nature works. The alternative isn't workable. If the universe did not have creative forces simultaneously opposing the force of decay, or entropy, there would be no universe.

Let's say only the evolutionary, creative impulse existed in the universe. What would happen? The cosmos would rapidly run out of matter and energy to use for new forms, since the old ones would never wear out or become obsolete. In personal terms, we speak of becoming an evolved person, but if you only evolved without dissolving the old person that you were in the past, you would be a perpetual infant, child, adolescent, and adult at the same time. Your body would have countless layers of skin because old, dead cells weren't sloughed off; your stomach lining would swell grotesquely without the work of digestive enzymes that constantly devour it so that it can be replaced every month.

On the other hand, if only the impulse of inertia or destruction existed, the universe would rapidly burn itself out. Entropy would cause "heat death" in short order, as the cosmos devolved into a cold, static void. We need these two opposing forces, but that isn't an argument for dualism. In fact, it's a strong argument for wholeness, since it takes a larger perspective than that from either side to keep them in balance.

Your body is capable of going into hyperdrive when the stress response is triggered. A flood of adrenaline speeds up the heart, draws extra energy from the bloodstream, alerts the mind, heightens the senses, and kicks you into gear for fight or flight. But if the stress response goes unchecked, it will kill you very quickly, in a matter of minutes. This has actually been observed in patients who have spent a length of time on steroids. The drugs they take to suppress inflammation, for example, also suppress the body's hormone system. If you suddenly withdraw those drugs, the body has no ability to secrete the right balance of hormones. Therefore, you can walk up behind one of these patients, shout "Boo!" and send the person into a state in which stress hormones speed up the heart to a dangerous degree, often with fatal results.

At the ego level we constantly fool ourselves into thinking that being absolutely good is possible. Never again will we lie, cheat, feel jealous, lose our temper, or give in to anxiety. This intention never works out, because being good all the time is as rigid as being anything else all the time. There are moments when it's absolutely right and healthy to get angry or be afraid. The flaw in positive thinking is that you can't be positive all the time. It's sane to fight against dictators, oppose oppression in all its forms, tell corrupt power brokers that they are wrong, and on and on. Life presents challenges from the dark side. We don't have to demonize the shadow; it's the source of almost every challenge worth facing.

The illusion that we fall into is thinking that life forces us to choose between good and evil. In reality there's a third way, which is to be whole. From the perspective of wholeness, you can balance the darkness and the light, being a slave to neither. The opposition between the two can be turned into creative tension. The good guys have to keep winning, but the bad guys better not lose altogether, because that would be the end of the story. The universe would become like a museum, fossilized and mummified forever.

The ideal is that the forces of truth, goodness, beauty, and harmony stay a step ahead of the dark forces. Your body manages to achieve that, as does the universe as a whole. We can't deny the fact that life-forms are constantly evolving, moving to higher levels of abstraction, creativity, imagination, insight, and inspiration. Something is maintaining the balance, but tipping it slightly in favor of evolution. In many ways, spirituality does no more than imitate nature. If you can help tip the balance toward evolution rather than entropy and decay, you are a true spiritual warrior.

Wholeness Is Close, Not Far Away

There is a map of human consciousness that holds true in every wisdom tradition. In this map a timeless God serves as the source of creation. Even when the word "God" isn't used, as in Buddhism, there is a state without division; it is whole; it contains everything both visible and invisible. The undivided state of Being then divides itself into the visible and invisible aspects of creation. Out of itself, oneness creates the many. You can imagine the map as a circle with a point in the middle. The point represents God as the source, which is smaller than the smallest particle of anything. The circle also represents God, but God as the manifest universe, which is larger than the largest anything.

But for the map to be accurate, you must see the circle as constantly expanding, like the universe after the big bang. Unlike the physical cosmos, though, God expands at infinite speed in all directions. This signifies the limitless potential of Being once it enters creation. So far, the map may seem esoteric, and many people would not see much practical value in it. (I once had a woman say to me that she was repelled by the words "One" or "All" as applied to God. To her, they signified being swallowed up in a sea of blankness, a divine void.) Our minds can't grasp infinite expansion in all directions. But make the map personal. See your source as a point while your whole world is an expanding circle. The more you see, understand, and experience, the bigger the circle gets. Yet it is always expanding from the source. What this means is that the source is never far away. It's a constant.

When you can experience yourself as your source and your world at the same time, you have become whole. The reason that your source seems far away is that you have identified with all the separate things in your world, neglecting the creative origin that makes everything possible. (This is like forgetting your mother as you grow up. No amount of forgetting will erase the fact that you had a mother who was your source.) It isn't possible to lose the connection to your source entirely, because consciousness is what the source is made of. Being aware that you are alive means that you are connected to consciousness. This makes the connection sound passive, however, and it isn't. Through this connection pours every thought you've ever had. There's also a silent side to consciousness that works to keep you alive physically. Your heart is aware of what your liver is doing, not in words but through messages encoded in chemicals and electrical signals. Your body requires an infinite range of responses to be coordinated among hundreds of billions of cells. This is an aspect of consciousness that never gains a voice, but its intelligence far surpasses that of any genius.

Ordinary people worry that God may be so far away that he has forgotten us, while religious enthusiasts fervently believe that God is close at hand every moment. Both views have a flaw. "Near" and "far" are actually false terms. They derive from duality, since near is the opposite of far. But imagine the color blue. Before you saw it in your mind, was the color blue close to you or far away? Say the word "elephant" to yourself. Before you brought it to mind, was your vocabulary far from you or nearby? We use consciousness for individual reasons, in the service of "I, me, and mine," but you can locate yourself in time and space without being able to locate your consciousness. There is no distance between you and a memory, you and your next thought. From the perspective of wholeness, since everything is being coordinated at once, distance isn't relevant.

Which leads to an exciting conclusion: your potential for change isn't far away, either. Potential is the same as unseen possibilities. Either you see that something is possible or you don't. So the impossible is just another name for the unseen. Thus the shadow, which makes you see a limited, fearful world full of threat and dark possibilities, is masking many unseen possibilities that could spring into your awareness if you expanded beyond the shadow. Without expansion you are forced to have narrow vision. Think of having a bad toothache. The pain occupies your whole attention; you can't think of anything else. If the human race were in constant physical pain, consciousness would never have expanded. Fear is anticipated pain, and it has the same effect of narrowing your awareness. Wholeness, it turns out, is the same as finding your source. There is no division at the source. You don't have to conquer every aspect of yourself that is tinged with darkness (which would be impossible in any case). Become who you really are, and from that moment on darkness is no longer anything you can identify with.

You are living near the source of consciousness when the following are true:

You are at peace.

You cannot be shaken from your center.

You have self-knowledge.

You empathize without judgment.

You see yourself as part of the whole.

You are not in the world. The world is in you.

Your actions spontaneously benefit you.

Your desires manifest easily, without friction or struggle.

You can perform intense action with detachment.

You are not personally invested in any outcome.

You know how to surrender.

The reality of God is visible everywhere.

The best possible time is the present.

Wholeness Is Beyond the Shadow

Human beings have fought against the shadow for untold centuries, but as far as I have ever discovered, it has never been defeated. The only ones who conquer the shadow don't fight it; they transcend it. When you transcend, you go beyond. In everyday life we transcend all the time. For example, when a mother sees her young child being cranky and demanding, she doesn't meet the child on those grounds. She realizes that he's tired and needs to sleep. What has she done? She has transcended the level of the problem, moving to a different level to find the solution. This gives rise to a spiritual truth: *the level of the problem is never the level of the solution.*

Instinctively we know this, yet applying it brings us to grief. Our fantasies force us to figure out which side is good and which is bad, in hopes that if we choose the winning side, victory will be total. It never is. Every dilemma has two sides. Every war fought in the name of God depends on an illusion, because the other side relies on God just as much. (Has any army adopted the slogan, "Victory is ours because God is not on our side"?) The enemies of transcendence play right into the hands of the shadow. You are choosing not to transcend when you struggle at the level of the problem.

Consider the following:

You have a chronic pain. Instead of going to the doctor, you take more painkillers.

You hear that someone dislikes you. You find reasons to dislike that person.

Your child is fighting with another child at school. You are certain that your child is in the right.

You hear that a couple is getting a divorce. You choose sides.

An evangelist comes to your door preaching a new religion. You slam the door in her face, because your God is the right one.

These are all instances in which the option to transcend has been rejected, and since these are such common situations, it's not hard to see how the shadow gains power. In each case, one side has been labeled good and the other bad. Someone is made wrong, so that you can feel right. Being judgmental is validated as a healthy way to view the world. The process of escaping the fog of illusion begins when you realize that no one is benefiting except the shadow. You will never be right enough, victorious enough, or virtuous enough to dispel the anger, resentment, and fear that are engendered in the

people you have made wrong. Once you see this, transcendence becomes a viable option. You start looking for the level of the solution
rather than the level of the problem.

Wholeness Resolves All Conflicts

I wish that the word "transcend" didn't come loaded with mystical
connotations. When you realize that you can "go beyond" in any situation, transcending comes down to earth. Conflict is the nature of
duality. Resolving conflicts is the nature of wholeness. This is only
natural. When you aren't just black or white, good or bad, light or
dark, but both sides at once, conflict melts away. The first step is the
most important. Shift your allegiance away from duality. Quit label-
ing, blaming, and judging. Give up fantasies of showing the world
that you are right and others are wrong. Spiritual teachers have of-
fered this advice for centuries. Remember what the Vedas proclaim:
"You are not in the world. The world is in you." Jesus taught that the
kingdom of heaven is within. There has been no lack of teachings
about the path to unity.

But people don't heed these teachings, because the invisible world
holds too much influence, much of it dark. Wholeness isn't real until
the hidden conflicts in your life are resolved. Let me outline these
conflicts in ascending order, beginning at the most basic level, such
as what a helpless child might experience. Each conflict becomes
more difficult than the one before, until we reach the level of spiritual conflict, which is like a war inside your soul:

The conflict between being safe and being unsafe.

The conflict between love and fear.

The conflict between desire and necessity.

The conflict between acceptance and rejection.

The conflict between the One and the many.

These conflicts ensnare everyone, extending far beyond the individual. Think of the countries that proclaim peace, but feel so unsafe that their real energies go to armaments and defense. They haven't resolved the basic problem of how to feel safe. Think of the times you have wanted to express love to someone, but felt afraid and vulnerable. You are in the same position as warring factions in a civil war who cannot embrace each other as one people. Conflict is entangled in everything, from relationships to international diplomacy.

Safe Versus Unsafe

The solution: Be established in your true self.

What does it take to feel safe in an uncertain world that is beyond your control? The great sages and teachers based their answer on the fundamental axiom that duality is unsafe and wholeness is safe. This is one of the great forgotten lessons. Many people work desperately to be safe by building up their defenses. They wall themselves off from the scarier elements of society. They cushion their existence with money and possessions. They lock the doors and pray that some unseen catastrophe doesn't strike. These tactics derive from a primitive belief that says that if your body is safe from harm, you are safe. Perhaps we inherited this predisposition; perhaps it suits our materialistic way of life. People in past ages didn't feel safe unless the gods, or God, approved their actions. To that end, they would tolerate being impoverished as long as organized religion told them that their souls were assured of salvation.

The modern view is that safety is psychological. To be safe in the world, you must find the inner key to safety. Houses, money, and possessions are irrelevant. In fact, some of the most insecure people are the ones who feel driven to excesses of wealth and success. The key to feeling safe psychologically is elusive. Freudian psychology holds that parenting in the first three years determines how safe a child feels growing up. Jungian psychology holds that feeling unsafe must be rooted in the collective psyche and specifically in the shadow, with its shared fund of fear and anxiety. But if you look at the results of a century of therapy, the psychological answer has barely worked in either case. So much insight and brilliance led to little more than the rise of Prozac and a generation of therapists who spend most of their time writing prescriptions for drugs.

You will feel safe when you discover that you have a core self. It exists at your source, as we saw previously. At the source there is no division, and therefore the external world can't threaten the inner world. Anxiety needs an external focus, whether it's the memory of some past trauma or a free-floating fear that creates dread simply because what comes next is not known. Your core self is stable and permanent; therefore it has nothing to fear from change. The unknown is necessary for change. When you make peace with that fact, the world will transform itself from a place of constant risk to the playground of the unexpected.

Love Versus Fear

The solution: Align with love as a force within.

Once you feel safe, you know that you have a right to be here. In order to feel that you actually belong, however, you must feel loved. Love is reassurance that you are cherished. Its opposite, which many people feel, is that you are a random speck tossed about in a chaotic world. The only sane reaction to that situation is fear. Religion has made stabs at offering complete and ultimate reassurance that God loves each of us, but at the same time it clings to the image of a fearsome, vengeful God. The reason that this duality is never resolved isn't mysterious. No one will ever meet God and ask if God really loves us or despises us, if God wants us saved or damned. From Moses to Muhammad, the divine has been confronted and asked that very question. The answer always seems to be both.

To escape fear, trusting in a loving God won't work, because that is either an intellectual choice, which is always open to doubt, or an emotional one, which is always open to hurt. As long as you can doubt or be hurt, naturally divine love will seem untrustworthy. Yet in consciousness we are able to experience the flow of love as a constant force, not a personal whim of the deity. The ancient *rishis* of India affirmed that bliss (*ananda* in Sanskrit) is not gained or lost. It is built into the nature of consciousness. Bliss in its purest form is ecstasy, joy, rapture. But consciousness unfolds from unmanifest and invisible to manifest and visible. As this unfoldment happens, bliss becomes an aspect of nature that has many qualities:

Bliss is dynamic—it moves and changes.

Bliss is evolutionary—it grows.

Bliss is pervasive—it wants to enter everything.

Bliss is desirous—it seeks fulfillment.

Bliss is inspiring—it increases by creating new forms to inhabit.

Bliss is unifying—it shatters boundaries of separation.

In the West we ascribe these qualities to love, which is bliss under another name. Love makes two hearts one. Love inspires great poetry and works of art. It breaks down the barriers between people. There is a tradition that venerates love going back as far as the records of time. Yet there is no doubt that we live in a loveless age, thanks to skepticism and materialism. Neither force set out to renounce love, but they have reduced love to brain chemicals, psychological conditioning, good or bad parenting, and mental health. None of these things are wholly negative; they lead to valuable insights. For good or ill, however, the tradition of exalting love as holy has been greatly weakened. What is left is that each person must discover whether the force of love can be experienced; seeking love has become another form of spiritual seeking.

I am fond of technology and gadgets, one of which is Twitter. I began to send and receive tweets by the hundreds, and the whole activity became seductive. One day I was tweeted with a question: "I'm looking for love. How can I find the right one? Does he even exist?" Immediately I tweeted back, "Stop looking for the right one. Be the right one." It was an instinctive reply, and I was amazed to discover that my answer was retweeted (i.e., forwarded) to two million people. The reason this seemed like such a novel answer, I came to realize, is that love has become such a problem that people genuinely are baffled about where it exists. A reply that seemed natural to me was exotic to many others.

What does it take to *be* the right one, which means to find love within? It takes the absence of fear. Love doesn't need seeking. Like the air you breathe, it exists as part of nature; it's a given. Yet, like any aspect of your core self, it can be masked. In fact, external love is often irrelevant. Someone who is depressed and anxious or who has a damaged sense of self won't respond easily (sometimes not at all) to loving gestures from another person. To find love, you must be capable of seeing yourself as lovable. The core self takes a simple view— "I am love"—because at the source that is exactly who you are. But in a world of conflicting values, this simple statement becomes confused and complex. The fog of illusion creates fear. Remove the fear, and what remains is love.

Desire Versus Necessity

The solution: Choiceless awareness.

"It has to be this way." How many times have you heard these words or thought them to yourself? Life presents us with impasses. We want to do something, but the way is blocked. Perhaps someone with an inflated ego says, "My way or the highway." More often, two people are stuck because they can't communicate. At one extreme is psychological compulsion, such as phobias ("I'm too afraid to do X") and obsessions ("I can't get my mind off Y"). These look like very different situations. A husband who refuses to go to a marriage counselor doesn't obviously resemble a phobic who can't stand heights or an obsessive-compulsive who washes her hands twenty times a day. But there is a common denominator. Each of them is trapped between desire and necessity. The result is also the same: they are no longer free to choose.

Endless energy is wasted trying to get past impasses. We call upon mediators, negotiators, and judges to settle disputes, yet in the final wash the party who loses always feels aggrieved. The conflict may be resolved on the surface, but not underneath. We go to doctors and therapists in the hopes that some illness can be diagnosed and treated. Here at least there's a chance of looking deeper. Yet the diagnosis is usually much easier to find than the treatment. Prozac and related antidepressants have proved effective in quelling the symptoms of obsessive-compulsive disorder (OCD), but not in actually healing the underlying condition, which returns if the patient goes off medication.

Yet no matter how skillful you are at negotiating, no matter how tactful and empathic you happen to be, the conflict between desire and necessity can't be totally resolved. Life itself presents situations where you can't get what you want. Not everyone marries the man or woman of their dreams. Failure in business is always possible. Winning is kept out of one's grasp. To a pessimist, there are more frustrations inherent in life than satisfactions. The sages and guides in every wisdom tradition have seen that desire is often blocked. It's surprising, then, that the Vedic tradition of India hardly ever touches upon resignation, patience, and self-sacrifice as virtues. Instead, the deepest wisdom of India teaches that there is a state known as "choiceless awareness." At first sight this seems synonymous with giving up. You don't make a choice, you give up taking sides.

We need to be clear: choiceless awareness isn't about giving up on what you want. It's about shifting your allegiance away from what the ego wants to what the universe wants. In choiceless awareness you let consciousness make all the decisions. In other words, the thing you want is also the best thing you could want. In such a state of awareness, according to the ancient *rishis*, there is no resistance from inside or out. Nature upholds your desires through a cosmic force known as *dharma*. It is a very fluid term. To the average person in India, to be in your *dharma* means that you have found the right work and manage to do the right thing in your behavior. *Dharma* is virtue or right living. At a deeper level, being in your *dharma* means that you are on the correct path spiritually. You are following the precepts of your religion and not falling into traps along the way.

But neither of these states resolves the conflict between "I want to" and "I have to." Desire and necessity remain at war. If anything, righteous people find themselves bound by far more duties and obligations than ordinary people, since religions of every stripe make many demands and attempt to curb all kinds of desires. Only choiceless awareness brings the conflict to an end, because when you reach this level of consciousness, what you want is also what you need to do, for your good and the good of the whole world.

In choiceless awareness, no one needs to tell you the rules of *dharma*. Instead, you have assimilated the *dharma*—you actually live the axiom, "I am not in the world; the world is in me." To maintain such a state requires dedicated personal growth, but everyone has experienced times like the following:

You are carefree.

There is an absence of guilt and self-judgment.

You experience a feeling of rightness.

Outside conditions don't block you.

Other people cooperate without putting up resistance.

The fruits of your actions are positive.

Desire ends in a feeling of fulfillment and satisfaction.

As you can see, this is a special combination of ingredients. Yet when you align with the force of *dharma*, this is your normal state. It's not enough simply to get what you want. Many people, if they have enough power and money, can fulfill their slightest whim without much effort. But feeling satisfied and fulfilled is much rarer, and often the exercise of power and money only inflames a person's desires and leads to deeper dissatisfaction. You can't satisfy your ego by giving it everything it wants, because the ego's whole reason for existence is to accumulate. It wants more money, possessions, status, love, power, and on and on. The machinery is fixed in place; it runs on a set program that is all but impossible to rewrite. The desires of the ego are superficial. Your true self is without ego. You aren't aiming for gain; you don't fear loss. When you give of yourself, you aren't secretly calculating what you'll get in return.

We are fortunate that there is another way to view the world, not from the ego's perspective, but from beyond ego, where wholeness exists. As the ego's hold is weakened, there's a subtle fusing of "I want to" and "I must." To act as the *dharma*—the will of God—would have you act totally naturally. You're simply being yourself.

Acceptance Versus Rejection

The solution: Unbounded awareness.

Fear of rejection cripples millions of people. It makes unrequited love a tragedy understood in every culture. Spiritually, you cannot be rejected unless you reject yourself. I doubt that any message has been so misunderstood, for when someone else rejects you, the pain feels inflicted, and you are the victim. To unravel how rejection works, therefore, we need to look deeper into the whole issue of judgment. This isn't a new topic, yet there's something new to add. All judgment comes down to judging against yourself. Self-judgment takes many forms, such as fear of failure, a sense of victimization, a general lack of confidence, and so on. Much of the time there is only a vague feeling of "I'm not good enough" or "No matter how much I achieve, I'm actually a fraud."

Many people hit upon a false solution. They develop an ideal image and then try to live up to this image and convince the world that it's who they are. (Hence the legend of the perfect pickup line that always works on women in a singles bar, a desperate fantasy that one can connect through image alone.) An idealized self-image can be so convincing that you even convince yourself. How many investment bankers, in the wake of the reckless greed that nearly brought down the world economy in 2008, continued to see themselves as not just innocent, but superior to the disaster they set in motion?

An idealized self sounds like a model of acceptance. Listen to what it tells you: "You're doing the right thing. You're in control. No one can hurt you. Just keep being the way you are now." Thus shielded, you can hardly do wrong, and if you do, your misdeeds are quickly covered up and forgotten. The beauty of having an ideal image of yourself is that you actually do feel good about who you are. The image substitutes for painful reality.

As you would expect by now, the shadow has something to say in this matter. At regular intervals some icon of righteousness, usually a preacher or public moralist, falls into scandal. Invariably these individuals have committed the very sins they accuse others of, improper sexual misbehavior being the most typical. Cynically we imagine that these Elmer Gantrys are rank hypocrites, that they live out the sham of public virtue so that they can pursue vice in private.

In reality fallen icons are extreme examples of an idealized self-image. Their powers of denial were superhuman. The shadow couldn't touch them. Then when the shadow did surface, an enormous sense of guilt and shame surfaced with it. Once they fall, these professional saints indulge in extremes of public atonement. Even in contrition, nothing feels real.

If you pull back from the spectacle, however, the whole drama could have been avoided. An idealized self-image isn't a viable solution. Only true self-acceptance is, and when that happens, there is nothing for others to reject. This doesn't mean you will be universally loved. Someone else might still walk away, but if that happens, you won't feel rejected. It won't result in an emotional wound. How do you know if you are falling for a false sense of self, which is what an idealized self-image is? You will hold such attitudes as the following:

"I'm not like those people. I'm better."

"I've never strayed."

"God is proud of me."

"Criminals and wrongdoers aren't even human."

"Everyone sees how good I am. Even so, I need to remind them."

"If I don't have bad thoughts, why do other people?"

"I already know who I am and what I need to do. I'm not conflicted."

"I'm a role model."

"Virtue isn't its own reward. I want my good deeds to be validated."

Dismantling your ideal image of yourself is a challenge, because this is a much subtler defense than simple denial. Denial is blindness; the idealized self-image is pure seduction. The way out is to go past all images. There is no need to defend who you really are. Your true self is acceptable not because you are so good, but because you are complete. All things human belong to you.

The most important ally you have is awareness. Judgment is constrictive. When you label yourself or anyone else as bad, wrong, inferior, unworthy, and so on, you are looking through a narrow lens. Expand your vision and you will be aware that everyone, however flawed, is complete and whole at the deepest level. The more aware you are, the more you will accept yourself. This isn't an instant solution. You must spend time looking at all the feelings you've so diligently denied, suppressed, and disguised. Fortunately, those feelings are temporary; you can go beyond them. There's nothing to reject, just a lot to work through. This is how a figure like Jesus or Buddha could have compassion for anyone. By seeing the wholeness behind the play of light and dark, they found nothing to blame. The same holds true along the spiritual path you follow. As you see yourself more completely, you will have compassion for your faults, and that will lead to complete self-acceptance.

The One Versus the Many

The solution: Surrender to being.

Finally, we arrive at the war in your soul. At this level, the conflict is very subtle, which sounds odd, because we tend to think that the cosmic battle between God and Satan must be titanic. In fact, it's very delicate. As you get closer to your true self, you begin to sense that you are part of everything. Boundaries soften and disappear. There's a blissful feeling of merging. As beautiful as this experience is, one last resistance crops up. The ego says, "What about me? I don't want to die," like the Wicked Witch in *The Wizard of Oz*, whose last words were "I'm melting, I'm melting!" The ego has been incredibly useful. It has guided you through a world of infinite diversity. Now you are about to experience unity. No wonder the ego feels fatally threatened; it sees it usefulness (and its domination) come to an end.

The ego mistakes surrender for death. To be whole involves surrender. You give up one way of seeing yourself, and in its place a new way dawns. "Surrender" isn't a welcome word to the ego, because it connotes failure, loss of control, passivity, the end of power. When you lose an argument, aren't you surrendering to the winner? Of course. Any situation couched in terms of winning and losing makes surrender seem weak, shameful, depressing, and unworthy. These are all feelings at the ego level, however. Seen without ego, surrender becomes natural and desirable. A mother who gives her children what they need isn't losing, even though one could say she's surrendering her needs in favor of her children's. That would be a false perspective. When you give of yourself out of love, you lose nothing. In fact, loving surrender is like a gain. Your sense of self expands beyond ego-driven needs and desires—these can never lead to love.

Surrender is not of the mind. You cannot think your way there.

Instead, you must journey into pure consciousness, before words and thoughts arise. That's the whole purpose of meditation, to carry a person beyond the thinking mind, which means beyond conflict. It's easy to believe these days that everyone knows how to meditate. If you have tried to meditate and then abandoned the practice, I'd like to suggest that you return. Not all meditations are created alike. Perhaps you were taught meditation as a form of relaxation or stress release or as a route to silence. These are all real results, but they aim too far short. The most profound effect of meditation is to transform your awareness. If you aren't expanding in consciousness, the true purpose of going inward has been missed.

Which is not to label any kind of meditation as wrong. But there has to be an intimate rightness that suits you. I've seen people who evolved very quickly using a simple heart meditation, in which they sat quietly and directed their attention to their hearts, and others who benefited by quietly following the in- and out-breaths as they sat with eyes closed. Eventually one longs to experience the true self completely. This can be achieved by going into the mantra meditation that originated in Vedic India or the Vipassana techniques of Buddhism, to mention just two proven methods. Whatever you do, remain awake to your vision of wholeness. You don't want to turn meditation into another kind of conditioning, where your mind convinces itself that it is peaceful or has found silence when both are just pleasant moods or habits. (In his typically blunt way, Krishnamurti warned that the worst thing a spiritual path can do is deliver what you expect. Instead of reaching the truth, the path has simply turned you into a version of your old self, but "improved" by feeling and looking better.)

The shadow is a thing of denial, resistance, hidden fears, and repressed hopes. Therefore, if meditation is working, these things will begin to diminish. You should be experiencing the following on your spiritual path:

Life becomes easier, losing its struggle.

You feel and act more spontaneous.

The world no longer brings negative reflections.

Your desires are fulfilled more easily.

You find happiness in the simplicity of existence. Being here is enough.

You gain in self-awareness, knowing who you really are.

You feel included in the wholeness of life.

If these sound like ideal goals, they are also noble ones and fully attainable. In fact, if months pass and you don't feel these things increasing, you need to stand back and reexamine your path. I'm not implying that your practice is wrong or defective. There are lulls and delays in personal evolution for everyone, because some issues take time to work out. Much of this working out takes place out of sight, in the deeper reaches of the unconscious. Artists are well aware of this; their muse doesn't answer on a time schedule. On the other hand, there may be serious reasons why the true self isn't unfolding:

Excessive stress

Emotional pressures

Distractions

Depression and anxiety

Lack of discipline or commitment

Opposing intentions—seeking more than one way of life

The spiritual path delivers everything; it can resolve all conflicts. But we expect too much of it when we ask for a panacea. Spiritual unfoldment is delicate. It can't be reached when your mind is too agitated or your attention overwhelmed by stress and other outside pressures. In other words, wholeness is a cure-all, but not an instant cure-all. You need to prepare the right conditions for going inward. To that end, each of the obstacles I've listed has to be dealt with. Stress, depression, anxiety, and distractions won't suddenly end just because you sit down for half an hour with your eyes shut. I hope that doesn't sound too blunt, because when you take even small steps to prepare the ground for meditation, it yields results that cannot be had any other way. This is the royal road to consciousness, and consciousness is whole.

In Summary

I will end as I began, with a physician's instinct for diagnosis, treatment, and prognosis. The shadow has outwitted and outlasted many approaches, yet some people have succeeded, and not just the great names like Jesus and Buddha. The force of evolution is infinitely stronger than the obstacles that block its way. You only have to gaze around you at the natural world to see the proof that beauty, form, order, and growth have survived for billions of years. In dealing with your shadow, you are aligning yourself with the same infinite power. After all is said and done, the requirements are not complex:

1. Acknowledge your shadow when it brings negativity into your life.
2. Embrace and forgive your shadow. Turn an unwanted obstacle into your ally.
3. Ask yourself what conditions are giving rise to the shadow: stress, anonymity, permission to do harm, peer pressure, passivity, dehumanizing conditions, an "us versus them" mentality.
4. Share your feelings with someone you trust: a therapist, trusted friend, good listener, counselor, or confidante.

5. Include a physical component: body work, energy release, yogic breathing, hands-on healing.

6. To change the collective, change yourself—projecting and judging "them" as evildoers only increases the shadow's power.

7. Practice meditation in order to experience pure consciousness, which is beyond the shadow.

I've laid out a vision of unity as the solution to the shadow. The instant that life is split into good and evil, the self follows suit. A divided self cannot make itself whole. There must be another level of life that is whole already. Casting their eyes over the invisible world, the ancient sages of India realized that it was indescribable. The Vedic scriptures from thousands of years ago were the first to declare, "Those who know it speak of it not. Those who speak of it know it not."

But of course people weren't thrilled to hear this teaching. They wanted help with their everyday problems. If a vision cannot be turned into practice, it's arid and useless. The ancient sages weren't trying to discourage their listeners. Quite the opposite, they were trying to give a reliable map, and where that map leads is to unity consciousness. My aim in this part of the book has been to draw the same map in vivid, modern colors. Now it's up to you to follow it. The shadow isn't a fearsome opponent, but a worthy one. Powerful as it is, the power of wholeness is infinitely greater, and by a miracle of creation it is within your grasp.

PART
II

Making Peace with Ourselves, Others, and the World

DEBBIE FORD

The story of the human being and the human psyche has been examined, studied, and written about since the beginning of our existence. Although it's been researched and dissected by brilliant thinkers, explored and explained by the greatest intellects of all time, most of us are still living in the dark, perplexed by the behavior of our friends, our family members, our idols, and—more often than not—ourselves. Disappointed by the condition of our own lives, we forge ahead each day hoping that our darker impulses and bad behaviors will miraculously disappear.

Hurt time and again by the flaws that we can't seem to shake free of, we silently pray that we will find the courage to give up our procrastination, our overspending, our chocolate, our resentments, or our sharp tongues. Yet we continue to succumb to our lower impulses, sabotage our own desires, and neglect our future. In an attempt to hide our discontent, we put on a happy face, muster our best "everything is fine" look, and continue acting out in ways that undermine our self-esteem and defeat our best-laid plans.

In the course of raising our children, chasing success, and struggling to put enough away for vacation or retirement, answers to the very questions that will help us grow elude us. Our deeper yearning for self-understanding gets buried beneath the daily news, family issues, a health crisis, or a common cold. An indignant neighbor, a disgruntled ex, or a child who has lost their way will literally suck the hours out of our days and the money out of our bank accounts while twisting our minds into believing that we can't and won't ever have everything we want. Sometimes, we even forget that we ever wanted anything different from what we have. The repetitiveness of our toxic memory can lure us into years of accepting more of the same and wasting away in a mediocre existence that fails to meet even our own expectations.

Unfortunately, this method of survival strips us of the ability to live the life that we were meant to live. The emotional pain that surfaces as part of everyday life has us wish away our past and become resigned about our future. If we feel we have been deceived or conned or that we have acted out of character, we become victims of the past and hopeless about what's to come. Cynical and skeptical, we fall prey to judgment, opting to point our finger at others rather than look inside ourselves for the answers to our woes. The robotic nature of our egocentric self rises up to help us overcome our feelings of insecurity and shame by protesting our innocence and proclaiming our differences. We think that if only we could just get that one person or thing to change, we would feel better. We believe that if we handle the one issue that we keep complaining about or get that one thing that we've been striving for, we will be happy. Rather than taking the time to pierce the veil between who we think we are and who we really want to be, we allow the illusional life of a self that exists in our minds to be in control.

The problem with this approach to life is that it prevents us from discovering our true self, and it endangers the areas of our lives that are most important to us. When we are busy protecting ourselves from the demons that lurk in the dark, we miss out on feeling joyful, fulfilled, and deeply connected with those we love. Intent on hiding the darker half of our human nature, we fail to reach our full potential and experience the depth and richness of our lives.

We were born whole, and yet most of us are living as partial human beings. We each have the capacity to be an important part of a grander whole. We have the capacity to leave this world a better place than we found it. We are meant to discover our authentic nature—the state of being in which we are inspired by ourselves, turned on, lit up, and excited about who we are. We are meant to overcome adversity and manifest the greatest version of our own individual soul, not a version of a self that is birthed out of a fantasy. Big, blown-out fantasies about our lives stem from the pain of our unrealized potential, but true dreams are a reality we are willing to work for, fight for, stay up late for—this is a future that is within our reach. And there is only one thing that can rob us of that future, and that is our shadow—our dark side, our secrets, our repressed feelings, and our hidden impulses.

The great Swiss psychologist C. G. Jung tells us that our shadow is the person we would rather not be. The shadow can be seen in the person in our family whom we judge the most, the public official whose behavior we condemn, the celebrity who causes us to shake our head in disgust. If we understand this correctly, we come to the startling and sometimes sobering realization that our shadow is everything that annoys, horrifies, or disgusts us about other people or about ourselves. With that wisdom in hand, we begin to see that our shadow is all that we try to hide from those we love and all that we don't want other people to find out about us.

Our shadow is made up of the thoughts, emotions, and impulses that we find too painful, embarrassing, or distasteful to accept. So instead of dealing with them, we repress them—seal them away in some part of our psyche, so we won't have to feel the burden and shame they carry with them. Poet and author Robert Bly describes the shadow as an invisible bag that each of us carries around on our back. As we're growing up, we put in the bag every aspect of ourselves that is not acceptable to our families and friends. Bly believes we spend the first few decades of our life filling up our bag, and then the rest of our life trying to retrieve everything we've hidden away.

Our shadow, filled with rhetoric and a hypocritical set of rules that we can never adhere to, leads us to glorify some and demonize others. It began with the teacher who called us stupid, the bully who taunted us, or the first love who ever abandoned us. We have all hidden away and repressed pain-filled, shame-filled moments, and, over time, these emotions harden into our shadow. These are the unexpressed fears, the horrifying shame, the gnawing guilt. These are all the issues of the past that we have never faced. Our shadow might stem from one defining moment, and most do, or it can accumulate over years of denial. As the shadow takes shape, we begin to lose access to a fundamental part of our true nature. Our greatness, our compassion, and our authenticity get buried beneath the parts of ourselves that we've disconnected from. Then our shadow gains the upper hand. It can trick us into believing that we are too unworthy, incapable, undeserving, unlovable, or stupid to be the superstar of our own life.

It is our dark side, the repressed and disowned aspects of our personality, that cuts us off our true self. The fact is that whatever we have hidden away in shame or denied out of fear holds the key to unlock a self that we feel proud of, a self that inspires us, a self that is propelled into action by great vision and purpose rather than one that is created out of our limitations and the unhealed wounds of our past. This is why we must explore our shadow. This is why we must unveil and reclaim our whole self, our true nature. This is why we must look within to examine the underpinnings of our life. Hidden here is the blueprint, a template, a vision of our authentic self.

My own study of the shadow began as I made the transition from a clumsy preadolescent to a pretty young teen. Confused and alone, I set off on a journey to fit in. I worked hard to feel good about myself, despite the fact that I was riddled with insecurities about everything from being a friend and girlfriend to being a sister and daughter. I fought to understand why I felt so bad about who I was. The voices in my head that seemed to overtake me—even at the young age of twelve—filled me with endless loops of dark thoughts and negative feedback: "Why did you say that?" "Don't be silly; he will never like you," "You're an idiot," "Don't stand too tall; people will be jealous of you," and on and on and on. I found it odd and confusing listening to these voices inside my head, because one minute they were telling me that I was nothing but a spoiled, rotten brat and the next they were convincing me that I was better, prettier, smarter, and more talented than everyone else.

An internal war raged inside my psyche. First it was, "You're great!" and then, "You're nothing but a little liar." "Everyone likes you because you are kind and warm," and a few minutes later, "You are a cold-hearted bitch who doesn't deserve to have any friends." These voices left me utterly confused about who I was. The coexistence of the positive messages and the negative warnings created so much havoc within me that I was either crying hysterically or going out of my way to spread good feelings to anyone who was willing to receive my love. They called it hormones at the time. Erratic behavior was expected of a girl my age, but mine was a bit more melodramatic, which earned me the title of the neighborhood drama queen. At last I had finally won a pageant, except this crown came with many negative projections from my family and lots of laughs from family friends who were privy to my private shame. I began to feel more and more powerless over my internal chattering, until I came to the conclusion that there was definitely something wrong with me and there was nothing that I could do to fix it. I tried with all my might to silence these voices, to make them shut up, by trying to convince myself that I was really okay. My moments of peace and happiness became less and less frequent, unless I was fortunate enough to be caught up in listening to a great song or playing with my friends. But in the quietness of a shower or an early morning rush to school, it became harder and harder to break free of the stranglehold of my internal demons, whose voices sounded like a church choir singing out of tune. Instead of feeling compassionate, kind, and gentle toward myself, I felt hopeless, hostile, and angry.

As my internal discomfort rose, I began to search for what might silence my ugly little mind and make me feel better about myself. My search for feel-good moments began with certain foods: Sara Lee brownies and a liter of Coke seemed to do the trick. I learned how to silently slip into my parents' room during dinner, go into their wallets, and steal the change I needed to get my daily fix. It started off quite easily, because the 7-Eleven was right across the street from our home on Forty-sixth Avenue in Hollywood, Florida.

As months went by, that fix was just not enough. The noisy, dark voices from inside somehow learned to slip through my sugar-induced feel-good moments. I had to find something else to manage these unwanted break-ins and put a smile back on my face—even if those smiles were met with the occasional internal voice threatening to "wipe that smile off your face."

My inner hunger to feel good soon became greater than my need to be liked or to be perceived as a good or "decent young lady." I was overcome with the impulse to change the way I felt. My sugar addiction quickly turned into something greater, as I picked up my first cigarette and a sampling of drugs. Pot, which was never my thing, turned into pills, placidillies, or downers, as they were called in those days. These escalated into psychedelics that led me to a plethora of other substances. As I succeeded in using drugs to create moments of complete peace—the mantra of almost every popular song back then—I ingrained into my young psyche a way of thinking and behaving that said to feel good I needed to look outside myself for something to make me feel better.

Over time I learned that the scary impulses that often came out in my behavior were not meant to be examined or expressed, but rather should be hidden and repressed, no matter what the cost. Slowly I slipped away from any semblance of the innocent child I once was and created an outer persona that exuded confidence and success. The more I played in the darkness of my own human demons, the stronger the impulse to hide my feelings of shame and unworthiness. I began to overcompensate for my weaknesses by becoming charming, friendly, street-smart, and savvy in the outer world. Although I struggled desperately in school, because I was too busy listening to the craziness in my mind rather than the teacher in the room, I wrapped myself up in a package that looked somewhat smart and pretended to be an opinionated know-it-all, hoping that I could fool everyone, including myself, into believing that I wasn't the dumb little sister of Linda and Michael Ford.

I watched what the rich girls were wearing, and either I begged my parents to buy me the knock-offs or I met with a group of kids at the mall on Saturday mornings to steal what I didn't have, so no one would find out that I was from a middle-class Jewish family. I didn't think being a Jewish girl was cool and had heard more than my share of nasty Jewish-girl jokes, so I studied how the town shiksas (the pretty non-Jewish girls—usually blonde) were behaving and took on some of their characteristics and behaviors as part of my carefully designed mask to hide my inner flaws and imperfections.

It was a game I didn't even know I was playing at the time. If I discovered something about myself that was not acceptable to my ego ideal, I would search the outer world to see who was acceptable, and with the sensibilities of a true artist I sculpted the new me, giving the illusion that I was the person I wanted to be rather than the person I feared I was. The problem was that no matter how much I over-compensated for the parts of myself that I feared or was ashamed of, in the silence of my own mind I knew the truth about who I was underneath my public mask. Although some could see through the glorious act that I had created, for the most part I had become a suc-cessful human being because I could fool those around me.

I tricked people into believing my smoke-and-mirrors act. I was able to enroll people in my happy life by smiling and spouting my many accomplishments of the day. Or I could invite them into one of my other favorite narratives—"Woe is me"—where I played the part of the damsel in distress. Either way, I became a master at hiding not just from others, but also, and most of all, from myself. I didn't know who I was or what I really wanted. I didn't know what truly made me happy or what left me feeling empty and devoid of emo-tions. My shadow was in control, even though, in all my arrogance, I believed I was the one in charge. Truly the dark side had won, until my persona came crumbling down.

Just like Humpty Dumpty, who fell to the ground, by the time I was twenty-seven I was stripped of my "I have it all together," know-it-all persona and left wailing on the floor of a drug treatment center. It was there that I came face-to-face with the real Debbie Ford—with all of her flaws, weakness, and disowned qualities as well as her gifts, strengths, and deeply hidden inner needs. It was there that I knew I was more than I could ever even imagine and that I was nothing but one of six billion human beings struggling to make peace with their dark side and their human vulnerabilities.

It was during this very humbling meeting with myself that I com-mitted to learning about who and what I was and why I felt com-pelled to do the things I did. It was at this pivotal time in my life that I began to understand the human shadow and the effect it had on my life and the lives of those around me—not as a theory in a textbook, but as a woman struggling to deal with her own unwanted feelings and deep insecurities.

Driven by deep feelings of loneliness that came from not understanding who I was or why I was here, I began my journey of becoming intimate with my dark side, my shadow self. This moment of reckoning became a catalyst for living a life beyond my wildest dreams. It has led me to study, grapple with, and dwell in not only my own human behavior, but the behavior of hundreds of thousands of people whom I have been privileged to guide into the territory of their unclaimed self and the glorious discovery of a life yet to be lived.

It is not my light that has led me to the wisdom I have shared in my last seven books, but my battle with my dark side (and the ultimate surrender in the war within) that has been my guide and continued inspiration. It is the very darkness that I spent the first part of my life running away from that is now my passion and my fuel to help lead others in this magical journey through the human psyche into living in the light of their greatest expression. It is a spiritual call, a higher voice that asks me to ask you: Are you ready to embark on this journey of reclaiming all of yourself, the light and the dark, your good self and your evil twin? Are you ready to return to the love of your true, total, authentic self rather than stay trapped in the judgmental angst of a disjointed human ego?

Becoming intimate with your shadow is one of the most fascinating and fruitful inquiries you can ever embark upon. It is a mysterious journey that will lead you to find your most authentic self—a place where you feel at home with who you are, where you recognize your weaknesses and your strengths, where you can bask in your gifts, admit to your imperfections, and admire your greatness. This self that is hidden beneath the mask of your human persona is the self that you are thrilled to be, a self that knows who it is and who honors the human journey. This self that you will discover as you embrace more and more of your hidden and disowned aspects is a self that offers you the confidence to speak your truth and pursue what's truly important to you. It's ironic that to find the courage to lead an authentic life, you will have to go into the dark rooms of your most inauthentic self. You have to confront the very parts of yourself that you fear most to find what you have been looking for, because the mechanism that drives you to conceal your darkness is the same mechanism that has you hide your light. What you've been hiding from can actually give you what you've been trying hard to achieve.

THE INFLUENCE OF THE SHADOW

From its invisible home deep within our psyche, the shadow wields enormous power over our life. It determines what we can and cannot do, what we will be irresistibly drawn toward, and what we will do almost anything to avoid. It explains the mystery of our attractions and our repulsions and determines what we will love and what we will judge and criticize. Our shadow influences what race or class of people we will approve of or relate to, whether we will be religious or an atheist, what party we will vote with, and which causes we will support and which we will ignore. It tells us how much money we are entitled to earn and determines whether we spend it wisely or piss it away. It is our shadow, our hidden self, that dictates how much success we're entitled to create or how much failure we're doomed to experience. The shadow determines the degree of care or neglect we give our body, the amount of extra weight we carry around our belly, and the level of pleasure we allow ourselves to feel, give, and receive. The shadow casts us into preassigned roles that we blindly follow in everything from work to love. Unbeknownst to us, the shadow is the author of a prewritten script that springs into action in times of fear, pain, or conflict or when we are just going about our business on autopilot. If left unexamined, our shadow will emerge from the darkness to sabotage our life when we least expect and want it.

Our shadow determines whether we will respect our children and trust that they will grow up to be independent, capable adults or whether we will try to mold them into everything that we are not. When backed into a corner, will we lash out in rage or will we withdraw into venomous silence? The shadow is an oracle that can predict all of our behaviors and reveal what makes us the people we are today. It decides whether we will be productive, inspiring members of society or invisible lost souls. When we expose our dark side, we understand how our personal history dictates the way we treat those around us—and how we treat ourselves. This is why it's imperative that we unmask it and understand it. To do this, we must uncover what we've hidden and befriend the very impulses and characteristics that we abhor.

Our shadow determines whether we will live a happy, successful, and stress-free existence or whether we will struggle with our finances, our relationships, our career, our temper, our integrity, our self-image, or an addiction. The *I Ching* tells us, "It is only when we have the courage to face things exactly as they are, without any self-deception or illusion, that a light will develop out of events, by which the path to success may be recognized." Only in the presence of an unwavering commitment to facing our demons does the doorway to self-discovery open.

We cannot journey into the dark side for a quick dip or an afternoon liaison. To understand our shadow completely takes a willingness to let go of what we think we know. It takes the force of a caged lion to break open the cellar doors that we ourselves chained closed many moons ago. The great news is that we were born with a burning desire to evolve and grow, to open up, to expand and be whole.

And I am going to assert that we all have at least one place where we secretly desire to be more, to have more, to experience more. It is here that our shadow is waiting patiently for us to come retrieve our power from the dark recesses of our unconscious mind.

When we first come in contact with our dark side, our initial instinct is to turn away and our second is to bargain with it to leave us alone. Many of us have spent vast amounts of time and money in an effort to do just that. Ironically, it's these hidden aspects and rejected feelings that need the most attention. When we locked away those parts of ourselves we didn't like, we unknowingly sealed away our most valuable gifts. The reason for doing shadow work is to become whole, to end our suffering, to stop hiding from ourselves. Once we do this, we can stop hiding from the rest of the world.

We must embrace our shadow in order to know the freedom of living a transparent life, so that we feel free enough to invite others into our life—to let others know the truth about our finances, our pastimes, and our relationships—without being gripped by the fear that our public persona will come unraveled, exposing the person we've been trying hard not to be. When our precious energy isn't tied up in hiding from or overcompensating for our self-destructive impulses, we are gifted with the clarity and the motivation we need to build an unshakable foundation for an inspiring future.

OUR DUALISTIC SELF

The shadow lurks, deceives, hides, and cons us into believing what we can and cannot do. It drives us to smoke, gamble, drink, and eat that which makes us feel bad the next day. Our shadow gives rise to the hypocritical behaviors that cause us to violate our personal boundaries and our own integrity. It is a force that can only be reckoned with by bringing it into the light of our awareness and examining what we are made of. We possess every human characteristic and emotion, whether active or dormant, whether conscious or unconscious. There is nothing we can conceive of that we are not. We are everything—that which we consider good and that which we consider bad. How could we know courage if we have never known fear? How could we know happiness if we never experienced sadness? How could we know light if we never knew dark?

All these pairs of opposites exist within us because we are dualistic beings made up of opposing forces. This means that every quality we can see in another exists within ourselves. We are the microcosm of the macrocosm, meaning within our DNA structure we have the imprint of every characteristic. We are capable of both the greatest acts of selflessness and the most destructive, self-punishing crimes. When viewed in the full light of our awareness, our shadow exposes the duality and the truth of both our human self and our divine self, as they both prove to be essential ingredients of a whole authentic human being.

We have to uncover, own, and embrace all of who we are—the good and bad, the light and the dark, the selfless and the selfish, and the honest and dishonest parts of our personality. It is our birthright to be whole, to have it all. But to do this, we must be willing to take an honest look at ourselves and step out beyond our judgmental mind. It is here that we will have a life-altering shift in perception, an opening of our heart.

The good news is that every aspect of ourselves comes bearing gifts. Every emotion and every trait we possess helps show us the way back to oneness. Our dark side exists to point out where we are still incomplete, to teach us love, compassion, and forgiveness—not just for others, but also for ourselves. And when the shadow is embraced, it will heal our heart and open us up to new opportunities, new behaviors, and a new future. When we bring our shadow, our hidden emotions and our life-draining beliefs, into the light of our conscious awareness, it will transform the way we see ourselves, others, and the world. Then we are free.

Dealing with our shadow is a complex but guaranteed journey back to love. Not just love of another, but love for each and every characteristic that lives within you and within me—a love that allows us to embrace the richness of our humanity and the holiness of our divinity. Having faced our own internal demons, we are filled with peace and compassion in the presence of other people's dark side. We can forgive and let go of our demeaning judgments and our resentful heart. We can tap into the humility of Gandhi and the tolerance of Martin Luther King, Jr., and draw forth the strength and the courage to deal with the issues that haunt us. "There but for the grace of God go I" takes on a whole new meaning when we can view evil through the universal lens of our humanity. Exploring our dark side is the gateway to understanding why we do what we do, why we sometimes act in ways that are contrary to the desires of our conscious mind, and why we spend countless hours, days, months, or years judging others and holding on to grudges that only bring us headache, heartache, and dis-ease.

All of us have moments from the past when our emotional pain was too much for us to bear, so we repressed it within the darkness of our shadow. This is an unavoidable part of life. We can run, but we can't hide. Our shadow is always linked back to one traumatic event or a combination of painful moments. When we truly understand our shadow and its gifts, there are no fingers to point or blame to cast on our parents, our teachers, or our past, because our shadow is a delivery system for an extraordinary future. Understanding how our shadow was formed unlocks the door to enormous personal power and profound wisdom.

THE BIRTH OF THE SHADOW

The birth of our shadow occurred when we were young, before our logical thinking mind was developed enough to filter the messages we received from parents, caregivers, and the world at large. Even with the best of caregivers, we inevitably were shamed for displaying certain qualities. We received the message that something about us was wrong or that in some way we were bad. As children, we might have been told that we were too loud. Instead of softening our voice, knowing there would again come a time to be loud, our fragile, unformed ego may have taken this comment to mean that our unabashed self-expression was wrong and should be hidden from others. Or maybe we were called selfish, because we took more than our fair share of cookies from the plate. Instead of understanding the cookies were to be shared, we made it mean that our selfishness was bad and should be destroyed. Or we got excited and yelled out an answer in elementary school, and suddenly all the kids were staring at us, laughing. Instead of laughing with them, we made it mean that we were stupid and we should never take a risk again. These negative messages got ingrained into our subconscious like a computer virus, altering our perception of ourselves and causing us to shut down those aspects of our personality that we or others deemed unacceptable.

Each time a behavior of ours was met with harsh criticism or senseless punishment, we unconsciously separated from our authentic self, our true self. And once these negative filters were firmly in place, we were separated from our joy, our passion, and our ever-loving heart. To ensure our emotional survival, we began the process of trying to cover up our true self in order to become who we believed would be an acceptable version of a self that would belong. With each rejection, we created more and more internal separation, building thicker and thicker invisible walls to protect our tender and sensitive heart. Day by day, experience after experience, we unknowingly constructed an invisible fortress that became our false self. This fortress of limited expression obscured our essence, hiding our vulnerabilities, our sensitivities, and often our ability to know and see the truth of who we are.

Before our malleable self hardened into a more rigid ego ideal, we had the freedom to express every aspect of our humanity. We had multiple emotional responses to any event in our life. Unburdened by shame or judgment, we had access to all parts of ourselves. This freedom meant that we could be anything we wanted to be at any given moment. There were no internal restraints to prevent us from stepping into the role of the sought-after object of attention or the jealous, wicked stepsister. Before we learned to judge one quality as better than another, we had unrestricted access to the full range of expression that resides within us. We could tap into elegance, grace, courage, creativity, honesty, integrity, assertiveness, sexiness, power, brilliance, greed, frugalness, laziness, arrogance, and incompetence as easily as we could change our clothes.

Life was a play when we granted all parts of ourselves the permission to exist. Each day was an opportunity for complete self-expression. And best of all, if we didn't like the way our story was turning out, all we had to do is go into our room, wrap a cape around our shoulders, bring forth a different character, and—voilà—we could rewrite the script and create a great new ending or even an entirely different story. We could turn a drama into a comedy or a boring epic into a fabulous adventure. There were countless possibilities, and we were curious to explore them all.

Once the shadow was born, however, our self-expression became stifled and more serious. We learned from our parents, teachers, friends, and society that to win love and acceptance we had to adhere to certain prewritten scripts. As we went to school, were exposed to media, and interacted with a wider circle of people, we observed that certain behavioral traits were demonized, criticized, or denied love and acceptance while others were idolized and showered with attention. From this time on, we distanced ourselves from any part of ourselves that did not fit into society's standards or our own ego ideals. We rejected more and more aspects of ourselves for all kinds of reasons—some because they seemed too bold, others because they were too silly or foolish.

We tried to figure out ways to get rid of these unwanted aspects of our persona until one day we got so distracted that we forgot they existed at all. With everyone giving us different messages about which of our many faces we should show the world, it became safer to listen to the voices of authority rather than trust in our authentic nature. Soon we found ourselves with only a limited range of emotions. Our self-expression was stifled; the endless possibilities that were once in front of us narrowed to just the few. We learned how to shut off life and actually became comfortable doing it. Eventually we identified with the internal character we believed to be most acceptable to those around us—and chances are we are still playing some version of that role to this day. We may make little changes here and there, but when we take an honest look, we may see that we've never really reinvented ourselves completely. Chances are we're like most people—we fix ourselves up a bit, put a patch over the parts of our lives that aren't working, and create a slightly new version of who we've been. By the time we move through our thirties, most of our choices are already predetermined in one or more areas of our life. Even the clothes we wear, the foods we eat, the types of entertainment we seek. The things we fantasize about are even repetitive and monotonous.

As we become more present and aware, we begin to see how robotic and trapped we really are inside the personas we've created. And we can choose to take proactive measures to deal with the shadows that are keeping us bound and try to break free. If we don't deal with these shadows, make no mistake—they will deal with us. They will show up in our relationships and separate us from those we love, keep us tied to a job or lifestyle that we outgrew years ago, or lead us to an addiction or habits that undermine our success and happiness. They will blind us from seeing the warning signs of an abusive relationship or a bad business deal. They will keep us in a state of perpetual denial, and in that state we fail to help those we love when they most need us, when they are faced with their own demons.

Every one of us has constructed an ego-based identity in which we have assigned ourselves an acceptable role that eventually smothers our full self-expression. Rather than being who we really are, we become a characterization of the person we think we "should" be. Over time, our stifled self-perception becomes the perfect breeding ground for our shadows to take root. Whether this role was created to compensate for some inadequacy that we believed existed within ourselves or as a strategy to meet the expectations of our parents, caregivers, or friends—if we strive to fulfill our ego's role to the exclusion of all other roles that we could potentially enjoy, we end up creating a life devoid of depth, adventure, meaning, and flavor. As we begin taking our assigned roles too seriously, they get sealed into our ego structure. Rarely do we deviate from the identity we've created, because we fall into the illusional state of denial and start to believe we *are* that identity. Looking around our own lives, most of us can recognize the limitations and repetitiveness of the roles we play.

Of course, it's much easier to spot the roles that our friends and family members are playing than it is to spot our own. We can identify the martyr who will volunteer at the PTA and take on more than her fair share of the workload (and then complain about it later), or the neighborhood charmer who is pretending to be superdad while secretly cheating on his wife. We know who likes to play the part of the gossip whore, who knows the dirt about everyone and everything (and looks for every opportunity to share it). We are familiar with the local drama queen, who is always being victimized in one way or another (whether it's by getting in a fender bender or because her husband didn't bring home enough money last month). It's easy to spot the eternal optimist who is always the life of the party or the wallflower who always sits passively on the sidelines. What's incredible is that even if the role we've assigned ourselves is boring, miserable, repetitive, or joyless, we cling to it for dear life, all the while rationalizing why we can't be more than we already are or have more than we currently do. Unknowingly we are the ones who have typecast ourselves to play some version of the same character year after year and rarely—if ever—do we allow ourselves to venture into a role that we aren't familiar with or a level of self-expression we don't yet know.

If we operate inside the myth that we must squelch, kill off, lock up, and hide all of the qualities that make us interesting and unique, we forsake our right to experience passion and peace. The quest for the perfect life, the perfect role, and the perfect persona will always leave us unfulfilled—even if we attain it—for the simple reason that we are much more than the small handful of qualities that fit neatly into our ego ideal. In the process of trying to express only those aspects of ourselves that we believe will guarantee us the acceptance of others, we suppress some of our most valuable and interesting features and sentence ourselves to a life of reenacting the same drama with the same outworn script.

In this quest for safety and predictability, our range of self-expression shrinks and, with it, our choices. Who and what we will be tomorrow is usually some form of who we were yesterday, because we can only access the resources and behaviors of the self that has consented to be seen. In shutting out the darkness we fear lurks within us because we fear the destruction it might cause, we also shut off the competent, powerful, successful, sexy, funny, and brilliant parts of ourselves that are yearning for expression. This is the root cause of the boredom we often feel in some or many areas of our life.

As we sever our relationship with certain aspects of our personality, we deny ourselves access to stimulation, excitement, passion, and creativity. One of the most exciting aspects of being human is that there are literally hundreds of inspiring, useful, and powerful parts of ourselves lying dormant, aching to come out of the shadow and be integrated into the whole of the self. There is a whole array of wonderful feelings waiting for an opportunity to move through our body, bringing us new sensations and new levels of happiness, joy, and pleasure. We can't really enjoy the enormity of who we are, because we have forgotten who we are beyond the borders of our own restricted internal barriers and the constraints we have imposed on our emotional world.

To be reinspired in any area of our life, we just have to look to see which of our shadow aspects or characters have been driven out of sight, find safe and appropriate ways for them to express themselves, and invite them once again onto the stage. We must challenge ourselves to accept all the faces of our humanity; otherwise the characters that got booted off stage and are now repressed will become the silent orchestrators of our secret life. Only in the presence of our entire, uncensored self can we fully understand and appreciate our totality and our uniqueness. We must find a good use for every character, or we will remain at war within ourselves.

BEFRIENDING OUR SHADOW

To begin to grasp how essential the shadow is, try to imagine a story without any conflict or a hero whose virtue is never put to the test by a worthy adversary. The hero of any story could not exist if it were not for the villains that challenge the hero along the way. If what the

Eastern wisdom traditions say is indeed true, that "the sinner and the saint are merely exchanging notes," then the conflict between our higher and lower natures creates the tension necessary to propel our evolution as human beings. The same concept that guides good literature applies equally in real life: *heroes are only as strong as their villains.*

In the drama of our evolution, the shadow is the character of greatest interest. The shadow is only dangerous when we keep it locked away in the dark cellar of repression. That's when we run the risk that it will blow up in our face, derailing our diets, sabotaging our relationships, and killing our dreams. But if we allow our shadow characters to serve as integrated parts of our whole self—as colorful, powerful forces for the good—they will lead us to richer experiences, more genuine connections, more laughter, more authenticity, and honest self-expression. The battle with our dark side will never be won through hatred and repression; we can't fight darkness with darkness. We have to find compassion and embrace the darkness inside us in order to understand it and, ultimately, to transcend it.

In his influential book *The Art of War*, Sun Tzu suggests that "to know your enemy, you must become your enemy." In this case, the enemy is usually an impulse inside ourselves that we don't understand or don't know how to deal with. As long as we're denying, repressing, or minimizing the importance of this and other hidden urges, as long as we believe that our own dark impulses will never catch up with us or be exposed, their wisdom will continue to elude us. By actively finding the gifts and receiving the contribution our shadow is trying to make, we redirect its once destructive power into a force that can benefit our life. More than that, we become a role model for others to find healthy outlets for the parts of themselves that don't conform to society's script or to their ego ideal.

We can be saints by providing the sinners that reside within us the freedom of self-expression—not by indulging bad behavior, but by seeing how this impulse or quality could serve us or society as a whole. The more acceptance and safe expression we find for our darker impulses, the less we will have to worry about being blindsided by them. I know you might be wondering how a part of you that you fear and loathe could actually serve you, but I promise you as you go through the process, you will see that there are gifts to be mined in every quality, feeling, and experience.

Reclaiming the parts of ourselves that we have relegated to the shadow is the most reliable path to actualizing all of our human potential. Once befriended, our shadow becomes a divine map that—when properly read and followed—reconnects us to the life we were meant to live, the people we were meant to be, and the contributions we were meant to give. Embracing our inner beast is the ticket to freedom. It is the conduit for tapping into all our greatness. It makes our inner life rich and meaningful and our outer life more enjoyable. It allows us to bask in wholeness rather than be constrained by the limitations of a self that was created by smoke and mirrors. Why smoke and mirrors? Because if we have created our public image or persona out of only those qualities we have deemed acceptable, we will have left out some of the most important, potent, and flavorful parts of ourselves.

OUR SHADOW MASK

Uncovering the parts of ourselves that we learned to repress is the key to understanding why we enjoy freedom in some areas of our life and behave like a robot in others. It is fear that convinces us to wear one of an infinite number of masks to hide behind and to construct a persona—a costume, so to speak—to conceal all of who we really are. We work tirelessly to create an outer façade, so that no one will find out about our dark thoughts, desires, impulses, and history. It is the shadow of our past that drove us to create the face—the mask—that we show the world. Will we be a people pleaser, or will we seek relief from the world by being isolated, distant, and alone? Will we work tirelessly to be perceived as an overachiever, or will we be content to lie in front of the TV or spend hours searching Internet gossip sites? Our persona was not created by accident; it was created in order to camouflage the parts of ourselves we deemed the most undesirable and to overcompensate for what we believe to be our deepest flaws.

This false self is charged with one mission only: to hide all of the unwanted and unacceptable parts of ourselves. If we were wounded from having been raised by emotionally unpredictable parents, we may work very hard to portray an image that we are calm and in control. If we had a learning disability growing up, we might create a warm, overly loving personality, so others won't notice what we perceive to be our handicap. If we are ashamed of the fact that we were raised by a welfare mom, we might become a highly motivated worker who is always impeccably dressed and well-spoken. The public image we create is contrived by the parts of us that were hurt, confused, or full of pain. Although it may fool others and even us for a while, eventually we will be faced with the wounds that this mask was constructed to hide.

As a way to ensure that our flawed and imperfect self would not be discovered or exposed, we cleverly began to develop qualities opposite from those we were trying to hide. We worked hard to overcompensate for the parts of ourselves we believed were unacceptable, hoping to throw others off the scent or to rid ourselves of the bad feelings that were associated with them. If we were riddled with insecurities, we may have developed an arrogant, know-it-all persona to convince others that we have enormous confidence. If we felt like a failure, we may have surrounded ourselves with people who have achieved great things or exaggerated the scope of our own endeavors to appear more successful than we actually are. If we felt powerless over our life, we might have chosen a career or partner that would have allowed us to appear more powerful.

Our personas convince us that there is nothing that we don't know about ourselves—that we are in fact the person we see in the mirror and believe ourselves to be. But the issue with this is that once we have bought into the story of "this is who I am," we shut the door on any other possibility and deny ourselves access to all of who we can be. We lose our ability to choose, because we can't do anything outside the confines of the character we're playing. The predictable persona we've constructed is now in control. We become blind to the immense possibilities for our life. Only when we stop pretending to be something we are not—when we no longer feel the need to hide or overcompensate for either our weaknesses or our gifts—will we know the freedom of expressing our authentic self and have the ability to make choices that are based on the life we truly desire to live. When we break out of this trance and are no longer preoccupied with fitting in, with what other people think of us or what we think about ourselves, we can open up and take advantage of opportunities that might just pass us by when we are trapped inside our story line or behind the mask we wear.

We are driven to the point of exhaustion by our ego ideal to be different than we are. We fight to be bigger, stronger, tougher, and more secure. Without realizing it, we position ourselves to prove that we are more, better, or different than the rest of the crowd or try to stay invisible by fitting in and not being seen. We scramble to create the exact persona we believe will bring us the approval and recognition we desperately need or, alternatively, give us an excuse for not playing full out and having a life we love. And then we begin to act and behave in ways, consciously or unconsciously, that will leave others with the thoughts, feelings, and impressions we believe will bring us their love, respect, or pity—until that one day when the walls come crumbling down.

Amanda was deeply ashamed of the fact that she never graduated from college and mortified that most of the relatives on her mother's side of the family were from the wrong side of the tracks and uneducated. She worked hard to create a persona to hide her embarrassment and make her look good to those she wanted to impress. She found a niche for herself in a specialized field where she was regarded as smart, helpful, and indispensable, but no matter how much she read or how much she contributed at work, Amanda ended most days feeling "less than." In an attempt to resolve her pain, she decided to go back to school, hoping that earning a degree would transform her from an uneducated girl from a trailer park into a sophisticated, worldly woman.

One evening she walked into her psychology class suited up inside her professional persona. She felt proud, because she had already created a reputation for being the smart girl in the class. As the professor detailed their assignment for the week, Amanda began to cringe as her shame-filled shadow took over. She could feel her whole body tightening up as she learned that the project was to create a very detailed family tree showing the educational backgrounds and careers of all her family members. As she began working on the assignment, noting all the members of her family who were drug-addicted, financially unstable, and uneducated, she was confronted with the pain and embarrassment of her family history. Her overwhelming sense of not being good enough suddenly felt too big to be hidden by any persona. Later in the week, as she read her report and looked over her comprehensive family tree, instead of feeling proud of the work she had done, she was riddled with shame. After years of trying to outrun her shadow and cover it up, it took only one assignment for Amanda's persona to crack open.

Like Amanda, some of us were aware, even at a young age, that we were trying to be someone we were not. Instead of ourselves, we wanted to be like someone we looked up to, so we unconsciously took on another person's façade, not even realizing that it was not an authentic self we were seeing. But either way, in our search for freedom, safety, and authenticity, it is imperative to recognize that we are wearing some version of a mask that we put on twenty, thirty, or even forty years ago. And now our authentic self, which is screaming to get our attention, is deeply hidden behind a mask, and our false self is masquerading as our true nature.

Imagine this. When you were a small child, you received a little gift—a magic penny, perhaps—from your grandmother. Wanting to keep it safe, you hid it somewhere so no one would find it. Would you be able to remember all these decades later where you had hidden it? Would you remember that you had hidden it at all? The same is true for your unscathed authentic self. You've kept it hidden for such a long time, you have forgotten that this part of you ever existed in the first place.

The nature of the façade we chose varies based on our background, our parents, our surroundings, and what was considered good and bad behavior, yet the masks that are commonly seen in our society today are no different from those of a hundred years ago. Today we see updated versions of the seductress, the charmer, the people pleaser, the eternal optimist, the "cool" one, the martyr, the good girl, the nice guy, the tough guy, the abuser, the bully, the quiet snake, the intellect, the savior, the depressive, the jokester, the loner, the victim, and the overachiever. They are repetitive, archetypal expressions appearing in the modern age. The problem with living inside these masks, these personas, is that eventually we lose sight of who we really are and what is possible for our life. In canceling out our darkness, we unconsciously extinguish our authentic power, creativity, and dreams.

EXPOSING OUR SECRET LIFE

Our shadow thrives when we have secrets. The moment we close the door on one or more aspects of ourselves, we set into motion a secret life. There's an adage in twelve-step programs: "Your secrets keep you sick." And in my years of working with people, I can confirm that this is, in fact, true. It is nothing to be ashamed of, because most of us have a public life and a secret life. We have a public persona we show the world and a secret life we keep hidden. We construct a secret life in order to hide the parts of ourselves that we're most ashamed to face. It could be an area of our life that holds some shame or where we are behaving in a way we fear will be unacceptable to those we love. Maybe it's an area of our life that's out of control, a habit or addiction we are struggling with, or a fantasy that we're afraid to speak out loud. When our behaviors are incongruent with the masks we wear, we will work hard to hide them. We might be really sweet and caring to everyone we come in contact with during the day and then go home at night and yell at our kids. Maybe we position ourselves as a brilliant intellectual while we're with our colleagues, only to go home and spend hours watching mindless TV and playing video games. Perhaps we're in a committed relationship but are secretly cheating, or we act like a self-made success when the fact is we are secretly living off our parents.

Our unresolved shame causes us to act out; it eventually gets expressed as an outer behavior that blows the cover off the parts of our life we've been trying to conceal. We can work day and night trying to control our hidden impulses from ever coming to the surface, but we are only a moment away from acting in ways that undermine our self-respect. If we've been hiding a part of our life in which we act without integrity, it will eventually be exposed as we write bad checks or cheat on our tax returns. If we routinely cover over feelings of loneliness, they may surface in the quiet of the night as an insatiable hunger for sugar, alcohol, or sedatives to fill the emptiness we feel. If the rage we were subjected to decades ago is not addressed and released, it may seek expression by turning us in to a nagging parent or a bickering spouse. Maybe our distaste for our cheating parent causes us to keep attracting partners who can't be trusted and are emotionally abusive. It could be that our normal sexual curiosity was shut down at a young age, giving rise to an insatiable fascination with illegal pornography or dangerous sex. However, to free ourselves from the unmanageable compulsions that cause us to live a secret life, we must find healthy ways to express our repressed aspects so that we can be safe from behaviors that can sabotage our life.

Matthew was the chief of staff at a prestigious medical university. He was admired by his colleagues and had a loving wife and three healthy children. Although to the outer world he looked like a pillar of society, he found himself bored with his intellect and all the accolades that came with success. One night Matthew returned home after making rounds and started watching late-night TV. He became fascinated by a young actress who was starring in a movie and decided to go online and check her out. One thing led to another and, while visiting a porn site, he clicked on an ad for a local strip club. The images he saw filled him with excitement. His mind began to wander, and he fantasized about stopping by the club on his next day off. Feeling a bit of excitement and fear, he rationalized his decision, reasoning that since the club was located on the other side of town, he could just put on a baseball cap and avoid being recognized by anyone he knew.

Soon visits to this strip club became Matthew's regular pattern. He found himself growing overly attracted to one of the women and eventually made a date to get together. The stories he told his wife became more and more complicated, with deeper and deeper layers of deception. He began looking for medical conferences to attend in obscure parts of the country, so he could enjoy a weekend of debauchery without worrying about being caught. As sex with his wife became less frequent and less exciting, he became more adventurous and started taking bigger risks. He even got into the habit of buying sexy lingerie and outfits he could take with him on his outings to ensure that his women could turn him on.

One weekend, Matthew's wife, Maria, took his car to drop their kids off at a tennis lesson, and when she opened the trunk to take out their equipment, she noticed a medical bag she had never seen before. After getting her kids to their lesson, she returned to the parking lot and—on an instinct—opened the bag. She was shocked to find sheer lingerie, condoms, and an assortment of other sexual paraphernalia stuffed in this small bag. Wanting to understand the extent of her husband's infidelity, she began looking through the credit-card bills, the Internet history on their computers, and his cell-phone bills. After studying his behavior for a number of weeks, she discovered just how big a secret life Matthew had been leading, which revolved around strip clubs, escorts, and countless one-night stands.

After several weeks of silent suffering, Maria decided to confront Matthew with all the evidence she had uncovered. With nothing to say and his hidden behaviors now out in the open, Matthew was faced with the task of unveiling the unfulfilled urges that had led him to create such a gap between his public persona and his private life. As the shock of the consequences of his secret life came into clear view, he was disgusted that his shadow had lured him into behaviors he never dreamed he would have been capable of. Like most sex addicts, Matthew needed help and soon discovered that it wasn't just sex he was seeking, but attention, admiration, and excitement. If he had been able to see and acknowledge these secret desires, he could have sought the support he needed before his behavior escalated out of control. Instead, his shadow caused him to lose his marriage and his dignity.

I have heard countless people in my seminars over the years share similar stories. Without thinking, they became somebody they never wanted to be. The bottom line is if we don't deal with our shadow aspects, our impulses and our repressed feelings, they will deal with us. As my friend Dr. Charles Richards tells us in *The Shadow Effect* movie, "Ignoring our repressed shadow is like locking somebody in the basement until they have to do something dramatic to get our attention." If we refuse to uncover them willingly, we put ourselves at risk of being in the line of fire of what I call the Shadow Effect. With no relief in sight for these repressed parts of ourselves, they take on a life of their own. By releasing the guilt and shame we carry when a part of our life is housed in the dark, we can instead open the cellar doors and exchange our secret life for an authentic life.

—

When we deny ourselves a safe outlet to express our dark side—or refuse to even acknowledge its existence—it builds up and becomes a powerful force capable of destroying our life as well as the lives of those around us. The more we try to suppress the aspects of our personality that we deem unacceptable, the more they find mischievous ways of expressing themselves. The Shadow Effect occurs when our own repressed darkness makes its presence known by driving us to act out in unconscious and unexpected ways. It occurs when something in the outer world forces our inner darkness out of hiding, and we suddenly come face-to-face with the character traits, behaviors, and feelings that we've kept hidden in our secret life. The Shadow Effect is not something we plan. In fact, it's something that most of us have invested a lot of time and energy in trying to avoid. But when we understand this phenomenon, we can unravel the mystery of our own self-sabotage.

THE SHADOW EFFECT

Imagine that every quality, every emotion, every dark thought that you try to ignore, hide, or disown is like a beach ball you are holding underwater. You take your selfish self, you take your angry self, your too-good self, your not-good-enough self, your foolish self, your conceited self, all the selves. And suddenly you're overwhelmed with all these beach balls you're trying to manage. When you're young, you have lots of energy, so you can manage a lot of beach balls—you can suppress a lot of your unwanted qualities. But then when you're tired, heartbroken, or sick; when you no longer believe in the possibility of an exciting future; when your defenses are down; when your attention is on your family or some big promotion you're going to win; when you've had one too many drinks—all of a sudden, boom! You or someone around you does something without thinking and one or more of your submerged beach balls pops up and hits you in the face. This is the Shadow Effect.

What is road rage? Is it anything more than a beach ball of suppressed anger forcing its way to the surface? We see it in the media all the time. A filmmaker making deep Christian films all of a sudden gets drunk and shouts anti-Semitic comments in a drunken rage. A radio star who makes his living being a great communicator in one second makes a racial slur that destroys his career and reputation. An ambitious young teacher throws away her future by having sex with a fourteen-year-old student. A movie star, with the means to afford almost anything, gets caught shoplifting. All of the suppressed impulses and hidden urges we have tried to manage are like ticking time bombs waiting to go off.

And what we can expect is that the Shadow Effect will arise at the least opportune time—when we're on the verge of financial success or in the midst of romancing a desirable new partner; when we're days away from retirement or about to close a deal that could change our life forever. These are the times when we consciously or unconsciously sabotage our own success; when one choice, made in the haze of unconsciousness, undermines the progress we've worked years to make. All self-sabotage is an externalization of the internal shame hidden in the dark recesses of our unconscious minds. Because we have not had the wisdom, courage, or wherewithal to make peace with what we have suppressed out of guilt, fear, or shame, it gets forced out into the open so that we can reclaim and embrace our lost self and return to the transparent state of our whole self.

It's not until our self-destructive behaviors are no longer a secret and we see through objective eyes the damage we're doing to ourselves and those around us that we find the motivation to change. It's not until our children come home from school to find the electricity cut off that we're willing to face our gambling addiction. It takes a DUI arrest to wake us up to the fact that our drinking has spiraled out of control. When we're out to dinner with friends and the waiter announces that our credit card has been declined, we might finally have to face the fact that our spending is out of control. When we get caught dipping into the company expense account, we finally realize that we must deal with our entitlement issues. We can fool ourselves that we are doing all right at work or on our diet—until we get our yearly review or step on the scale. The Shadow Effect arises as a potent outer reflection that our inner world is dangerously out of balance. But as painful as these moments of truth can be, they can serve to begin a process of involuntary evolution. When we are confronted with our shadow and it is seen by those whose opinions matter to us, we snap out of denial and hopefully recognize that we must do something about it.

If we were able to see ourselves accurately, it would be an easier task. But we can't, and because of this, it is so easy to fall into the trance of denial, otherwise known as "Don't Even Notice I Am Lying." The lie begins with ourselves. If we were intimate with our darker impulses—if we knew that selfishness, hatred, greed, and intolerance have an important message to deliver—we would heed their presence in our life, like a trusted friend knocking at the door. But when we alienate our shadow, when out of fear we refuse to acknowledge or receive the messages it is trying to send, we can be certain that we will do something or become involved in something that brings our hidden darkness to the surface. At these times, the proverbial knock on the door feels more like a knock in the head; yet the moments we meet our own disowned darkness are not only some of the most painful, but also the most fertile times of our life.

If we wish to avoid the wrath of the Shadow Effect, we must do a reality check with ourselves every day to see if we are acting in ways that could shame, embarrass, or destroy our family, career, health, or self-esteem. We must wake up and consider whether we are hiding and denying a secret life; we must become aware of habits, behaviors, or ways of being we are keeping from others. If we fear what would happen if our families, coworkers, or friends looked through our e-mails, checked the history of our most recently viewed sites on our computers, or read the judgmental, mean thoughts in our minds, we must recognize these as signs—as flashing red lights. Denial is the culprit that keeps our secret life intact and out of sight—and keeps us focused on anything but our own indiscretions.

To embrace our shadow and derail the possibility of the Shadow Effect taking us down, we must open up to a greater truth about our humanness and what lurks beneath the surface of the person we believe ourselves to be. When we engage our minds in investigating the hypocrisy of our human behavior, we open up to a deeper, more meaningful truth—that all parts of ourselves deserve to be seen, heard, and embraced, that every aspect holds a greater gift than we can see and every feeling deserves healthy expression. When they are taken out of the darkness and exposed to the light, they will support us in creating healthy relationships, regaining good mental health, and achieving our potential.

The Shadow Effect shatters our perfectly constructed persona so that we can reinvent ourselves as somebody other than who we've been. Self-sabotage is nothing more than an unwillingness on the part of our higher self to continue playing the role we have assigned to ourselves. Ideally, we embrace our disowned aspects willingly; when we insist on clinging to our personas, the fallout can be painful and messy. There are examples of this everywhere. Britney Spears, the all-American Mouseketeer who wore the good-girl mask, spirals into self-destruction and becomes a notorious bad girl. Tiger Woods, the all-star golfer with the nice-guy overachiever mask, acts out and in one day goes from a superhero to a self-sabotaging cheater. When the mask of our human persona gets too tight, when there is no more room to grow or breathe, it blows itself up, so that it can re-create itself anew. There are literally millions of examples throughout time that clearly demonstrate the phenomenon of the Shadow Effect. Yet when these little or massive indiscretions of others are brought to light, we are left shaking our heads, perplexed at their behavior. We call it a fall from grace, but is it really a fall from grace? Is grace no more than a well-constructed act we show the world, while our secret life is hidden from those we love?

UNCOVERING OUR SHADOW

When we find ourselves obsessed with aspects of other people's shadows, it is only because they have touched one of our own. We are used to thinking that we cannot see ourselves unless we are looking in a mirror—but this is true only on one level. The fact is we *can* see ourselves in living color by taking note of what we observe in other people. We are designed to project onto others the qualities we can't see in ourselves. It's not a bad thing. We all do it all the time. Projection is an involuntary defense mechanism of the ego; instead of acknowledging the qualities in us that we dislike, we project them onto someone else. We project them onto our mothers, our kids, our friends, or, even better, some famous public figure we have never even met. Whatever we judge or condemn in another is ultimately a disowned or rejected part of ourselves. When we are in the midst of projection, it appears as though we are seeing the other person, but in reality we are seeing a hidden aspect of ourselves. Those we project on hold pieces of our unclaimed darkness as well as pieces of our unclaimed light. Simultaneously afraid of our own unworthiness as well as our own greatness, we unconsciously transfer these qualities onto another rather than own them ourselves.

You have already experienced the power of projection thousands of times in your life. You walk into a room and feel suddenly enamored with someone. You begin a conversation, and then she starts telling you about her likes or dislikes that don't mesh with your own. Suddenly that person looks different to you—the trance of projection has been broken and you see her in a completely different light. If a moment later she happens to mention that she can get you courtside tickets to a game you've been dying to see or that she knows someone who can help you get your latest project off the ground, you may again see her in a favorable light and she may seem more interesting. Finally, the conversation is back on track, but in the very next breath she starts dropping names, and when she suddenly reminds you of your bragging father-in-law, you feel repulsed. In reality, nothing about this person has changed except your perception of her. This is the power of projection. If you understand this phenomenon, you will understand why you can love someone one minute and in the very next moment find that person unbearably annoying.

Our unclaimed darkness continually shows itself on the screen of those around us. We might see our submissiveness in our mother, our greed in our father, our laziness in our husband, or our righteousness in politicians. Projection sounds like this: "She's so self-centered." "He is so full of himself." "What an idiot. He is such a loser." Projection explains why five siblings can grow up in the same home, and each of them will recount a different story about their parents, assign them a different set of strengths and weaknesses, and remember them as possessing different characteristics.

It's often hard to recognize our own bad behavior, because we are continually projecting it on others. The more convinced we are of other people's wrongdoings, the more likely it is that we ourselves are guilty of the same indiscretions. A.J., who tends bar at a popular restaurant, was headed home after a long day's work and looking forward to spending a quiet evening with his wife and family. A few short minutes into his drive, he suddenly heard the noise behind him that we all dread—the squeal of a siren. As he pulled over, he searched his memory to see what he could have done, but nothing came to mind. He rolled down his window, and the officer asked to see his license.

After he handed over his ID, the officer leaned in and asked him, "Young man, have you been drinking?"

A.J. replied, "No, sir, I was at work."

"Young man, I believe you have been drinking, and it would serve your best interest to tell the truth. Maybe you've been somewhere besides work?" the officer asked sarcastically.

A.J., feeling agitated and slightly defensive, said, "No, sir, I haven't been drinking. Actually, I was at the sports bar serving you drinks all afternoon."

The officer, obviously stunned, handed A.J. his license back, got into his patrol car, and drove away. This is a perfect example of projection. When the officer, a little buzzed and maybe feeling a bit guilty about having a few drinks while on duty, went back to work after his "break," he unconsciously began looking for himself.

The parts of ourselves we try to avoid may be hidden from our view, but they exist as part of our energy field regardless. The behaviors and feelings we are not at peace with will always find a screen to project themselves on, and we can be sure this is happening when we feel an emotional charge in the presence of someone else. Imagine having a hundred different electrical outlets on your chest. Each outlet represents a different quality. The qualities you acknowledge and embrace have cover plates over them. They are safe—no electricity runs through them. But the qualities you're not okay with, the ones you have not yet owned, do have a charge. So when others come along and reflect back to you an image of a self you don't want to be, you become reactive.

Here's an example. I once dated a man I considered to be a bit chubby and out of shape. After a few months of dating, I noticed that, no matter where we went, he would point out the guy who was overweight, who had a pot belly, or whose pants hung too low. One day, as we were walking through the airport on our way out of town for a romantic getaway, he pointed his finger at another man he didn't even know and would never see again and said, "What a slob. Why do you think that guy doesn't take care of himself?"

I finally couldn't keep my mouth shut any longer, and I mustered up the courage to tell him that he was just projecting his own weight concerns on various poor overweight men he didn't even know. I suggested that instead of pointing his finger at them, he should just look down. I thought he was going to trip getting off the escalator as he spotted, as if for the first time, his own bulging belly. His face dropped as he realized that he too was carrying an extra twenty-five pounds of unwanted weight. Embarrassed, he sheepishly asked me if he really looked like the other men. Scared that I would ruin my fun weekend away, I lied and told him that maybe he wasn't as bad as the others, but that there were many other places his eye could be going when we were out in public, so it must mean that, at some level, he really wanted to take on his own body and alter the way he appeared in the world or he wouldn't be so plugged in.

There were literally hundreds of other traits he could have focused on—somebody's hair, smile, beautiful eyes, or big nose. But he didn't. He only focused on other men's bellies. Our projections always shock us. When we are judging another, we never really think we are talking about ourselves. But once we understand our finger-pointing, we can start to untangle ourselves from our perceptions and fierce judgments of others. We must remember the old saying, "You spot it, you got it."

If we deny or are uncomfortable with our anger, our eye will automatically search and find all the angry people. If we are secretly lying or judging ourselves for lying in the past, we will be righteously upset about the dishonesty of others. In my years of leading workshops, I've had some incredibly funny moments when people got mad at me for suggesting this very concept of projection and telling them that they too possessed the qualities they dislike in others. One of my favorites was when a beautiful Hispanic woman in her late twenties came up to me on one of the breaks insisting that she wasn't anything like her father, who didn't approve of the men she went out with. When I asked her if she knew why, she said it was because he is a racist. She said she only went out with Asian men, and he didn't approve of them. When I jokingly asked her what kind of Hispanic woman only goes out with Asian men, the anger drained out of her face, and she meekly suggested, "Someone who's a racist?" She realized in that moment that she was a bit of a racist, just like her father, because she would never go out with men of her own background.

Another woman protested that she wasn't anything like her judgmental father, who always pointed out what was wrong with her. She told me he was angry, hypocritical, nasty, critical, and so on. When I asked her what she just did to her father in the course of this conversation, she realized she was demonstrating the same judgmental behavior that she saw in him. Another time, a man stood up to tell me how much he hated closed-minded people and how he seemed to be surrounded by them at work and in his own neighborhood. Then one day, his beloved son came home from college and announced that he was gay. This man was filled with disgust. When his wife tried to settle him down, he realized that he was the closed-minded person he always despised, which led him to "The Shadow Process" workshop. Owning our projections is a courageous and yet humbling experience we all must go through to find peace. It forces us to acknowledge that we are capable of and often do the very things we dislike in others.

There are many famous examples of projection. The former governor of New York Eliot Spitzer spent his career trying to clean up prostitution, because he deemed it so unacceptable, and then got caught in a call-girl scandal. Former Speaker of the House Newt Gingrich, who continually pointed his finger in outrage and led the charge to impeach President Bill Clinton for sexual indiscretions, was later found having an affair outside his marriage. The famous preacher Reverend Ted Haggard, who railed about the immorality of homosexuality, was later caught having a drug-fueled homosexual relationship. And the radio phenomenon Rush Limbaugh, who on his radio show openly shamed and derided drug addicts, later admitted his own addiction to prescription medicine. I could literally give thousands of examples of people publicly demonizing and putting down behavior they are currently displaying. Do you think these people really set out to destroy their lives and careers, to publicly humiliate themselves and shame their families? Was this really their intention? Or were they in fact caught by surprise and deeply disappointed in their own behavior? Is "The Devil made me do it" really the shadow in disguise?

As Shakespeare so brilliantly said, "The lady doth protest too much." Whatever quality, behavior, or feeling we find ourselves righteously denying, we can be certain that is the one we are harboring deep within our own psyche. We don't have to look far to discover that we are usually doing the exact thing we are judging others for. It may show up in a completely different way, yet the driving force behind our behavior is, in fact, the same. It can sometimes be challenging to identify the driving force in ourselves, because we may not be displaying the exact behavior as the person we are projecting onto, but it is there within us. When we have a trait that doesn't have a cover plate over it (to use the earlier image of multiple electrical outlets), we draw people and incidents into our life to help us acknowledge, heal, and embrace that denied aspect.

If we embrace the qualities that disturb us in others, we will no longer be upset by them. We might notice them, but they won't affect us. Those outlets will have cover plates over them, so they will no longer carry a charge. It is only when we are lying to ourselves or hating some aspect of ourselves that we become emotionally charged from someone else's behavior. Revered philosopher and psychologist Ken Wilber makes a great distinction. He says if a person or thing in the environment *informs* us, if we receive what is happening as information or a point of interest, we probably aren't projecting. If it *affects* us, if we're pointing our finger in judgment, if we're plugged in, chances are we are a victim of our own projections.

Until we take back all the parts of ourselves we have projected away, whatever we refuse to accept will keep showing up in our life, either in our own behavior or in the behavior of someone close to us. When we don't deal with our shadow, it will negatively affect our relationships. It will rob us of being present to the gifts of those around us, because we will have put up a defensive wall of judgment that blinds us from truly seeing who others are. It will distract us from the relationship as a whole and, instead, force our eye and our attention to what we believe is wrong about others.

Pilar's behavior is a perfect example of the phenomenon of projection. A woman in her early forties who prides herself on being a good daughter, Pilar is constantly upset at her father for being a hoarder. As she drives over to his house each Sunday to visit him, she begins to feel anxious and annoyed. By the time she walks into his living room to settle in for their afternoon father-daughter time, instead of asking him how he is doing or updating him on her own life, she starts barking at him about all the piles of newspapers on the floor and the hundreds of little items of memorabilia scattered around his small living space. Frustrated by her father's inability to throw things out and listen to her direction to dump everything into the trash, Pilar engages in a belittling conversation in which she points out his inability to let go of useless items. Sitting in such an atmosphere of judgment, they both feel sad, and their visits end up being monotonous and life-draining for both of them. Pilar always drives away feeling bad about herself, and her father secretly wishes she would just stop coming, although he's too kind and lonely to say so.

One day while working in the home office she shares with her husband, Emilio, Pilar realized something about herself. Emilio asked her if she could empty one of the drawers she was using, so he could have more room for his papers. Annoyed, she quickly responded that she needed six of the eight drawers for all of her important papers and that he could rent a storage unit if he needed more room. Agitated at his wife's inability to share, Emilio began to yank open one after another of her cabinet drawers, revealing hundreds of files stuffed with newspaper and magazine clippings. She heard Emilio ranting, even though she was no longer listening to the content of what he was saying. She was stunned. Here it was right in front of her—her father's bad habit. She could see that to Emilio all these clippings were useless junk. She had saved some of these clippings for a long time, even coupons from when she was in college over twenty years earlier!

Suddenly, when she brought her mind back into the room where her husband was still arguing that she didn't need half of what was in the drawers, she began laughing out loud. In just a few moments, she went from feeling nauseous when her own shadow was exposed to being set free when she broke the trance of her projection. She saw how she displayed the same quality as her father, even if hers was hidden in closed cabinet drawers. She embraced the fact that she was a hoarder and asked her husband to please help her clean out and throw away some of her clippings, because she knew it would be difficult to do on her own. She loved all her pieces of paper just as her father loved his.

Days later when Emilio got not only one drawer but three, Pilar decided to share her story with her father and ask that he forgive her for being so judgmental. Both father and daughter had a good laugh together and hugged, which is something they did as a routine greeting, but never as an authentic expression of love and respect. Her own admission of guilt opened up a new loving and respectful relationship between Pilar and her father that allowed him little by little to let go of his past. He even allowed her to help him fill a few garbage bags each Sunday.

Here's what's so exciting. When you understand projection, you will never see the world the same way again. In this holographic world, everyone and everything is a mirror, and you are always seeing yourself and talking to yourself. If you choose, you can now look at what emotionally affects you as an alarm, a clue to uncover your shadow, a catalyst for growth that gives you an opportunity to reclaim a hidden aspect of yourself. Every shadow aspect you embrace will allow you to experience more love, more compassion, more peace, and a greater sense of freedom.

And there is even more great news about owning our projections. When we do, the people in our life experience increased freedom and have an opportunity to shift their behavior. When we disown qualities, behaviors, and feelings and attribute them to other people, those traits appear to actually exist in other people and not ourselves. But time and time again I've seen that when people wake up from the trance of projection, the people they have been projecting onto change—they become free to show up differently. When we can see them as they are, release them from our own judgments and clouded perceptions, a new reality will emerge. Ultimately, we must come to a place where we can uncover, own, and embrace every quality that exists, so that we no longer have to project our disowned aspects on others, so we can be free to see people through the wide lens of compassion rather than the illusional lens of projection. It is then that we will be free to love not only ourselves, but all those we see in the world. It is then that we will experience true freedom.

UNMASKING OUR SHADOW

Another effective way of finding unclaimed parts of ourselves is to explore the repetitive behavior patterns we have struggled with for years. These patterns of behavior, which stem from unclaimed and rejected parts of ourselves, become our nemesis. Often we trick ourselves into believing that our less than acceptable behavior is the problem rather than searching for the root cause of the behavior. We may spend years fighting with the same ten pounds, or cigarettes, womanizing, or overspending, only to find ourselves right back where we started or in an even worse position. But if we understand that our patterns of behavior were formed from repressed feelings or a disowned or shamed aspect of our shadow, we can go to the source of our behavior and dismantle the pattern.

All of our habitual behavior stems from an experience or experiences in the past that led us to create particular interpretations about ourselves. From those interpretations certain thoughts were born, and these thoughts made us feel a particular way about ourselves, often a negative one. Our desire to distance ourselves from these unwanted feelings drives us to find ways to make ourselves feel better; thus the birth of our self-sabotaging behaviors.

Annette was six or seven the first time her mom told her she was going out and leaving her alone for the evening. As the sky darkened, she wandered around the empty apartment and decided that her mom didn't love her. She was plagued by the thought that something bad would happen to her mom and she would be left alone forever. This caused her to feel alone, afraid, panicky, and, above all, different from the other kids whose moms stayed home and cooked dinner. To douse these feelings, Annette found herself taking multiple trips to the kitchen, where her mom had left a big pink box of donuts. She learned that, at least for a short time, the treats made her painful feelings not so bad.

If we explore our behavior patterns—especially those we don't wish to repeat—we always uncover a shadow aspect of ourselves that we are trying to hide or cover up. The repetitive patterns we find ourselves trapped in always echo back to us feelings that accompanied the original wound. Then, in a great cover-up, we create patterns of behavior that ultimately reinforce the wound rather than giving us the relief that we seek.

Helena was constantly overwhelmed and anxious, because she found herself procrastinating on work projects, tasks at home, and things like getting the oil changed in her car or making an appointment to go to the dentist. Every time she came face-to-face with the consequences of her procrastination, she made a strong promise to herself that she would change. Helena was clear that this pattern of behavior was emotionally depleting and debilitating. Filled with regret, Helena called me proclaiming that she just couldn't take it one more day. After listening to her rant, I asked her if she was ready to find the root cause of this pattern, the portion of the shadow that was robbing her of a peaceful and joyous life. With trepidation and a bit of resignation, she agreed.

So I asked my first question: What kind of person would procrastinate? Suddenly she saw an image of her stepfather lying on the couch with the television blasting; he was not getting his work done around the house, and her mother was enraged. As she located the root of the wound, she felt the embarrassment and shame of realizing that she carried that same undesirable quality her stepfather had. When I asked her what interpretation she made about her stepfather, she told me that she deemed him a lazy bum, even though he was very successful in his career. Helena, who was at that time just shy of her thirteenth birthday, decided that from that day forward she would never be lazy like her stepdad. In fact, those around her would say that just the opposite was true—that she was a doer, highly effective, productive, driven, and energetic. But Helena always knew what was left undone, waiting for her to deal with in her own life. She recalled the names she heard being shouted at her stepdad— "You're a good-for-nothing lazy bum!"—and easily identified the internal dialogue that plagued her on an ongoing basis; the demoralizing truth was that she was repeating these same words to herself more and more each year.

But now as an adult, she saw that even though she was extremely busy doing tons of things each day, she wasn't able to do what was truly important to the success of her own life. Even though she sat appalled for a few minutes at the thought that she might be lazy just like her stepdad, she could see that this shadow quality, which she had so masterfully hidden, had taken root in her own life and now had to be weeded out if she was to be free from this self-defeating pattern. It didn't take her long to accept the fact that, indeed, she was lazy when it came to herself. With the real source of her behavior now in front of her, she could begin the process of making peace with the lazy part of herself, so that it would not have to undermine her choices each day and rob her of her self-esteem and her dreams.

Every time we find a behavior that threatens our peace of mind, our happiness, or our safety, we are implored to heed the call of our internal world and explore the root cause of our behavior. When we do, we will unveil an aspect of our shadow. It doesn't have to take a year or a lifetime. It can take five minutes of radical honesty to unravel a pattern from our past. If we find an impulse in ourselves that we unknowingly hid, we have the right and the ability to bring it into the light of our awareness, forgive ourselves and others for the pain we experienced, and break free from the self-defeating behavior.

Maybe self-neglect is a pattern of behavior that you must confront. You show up for others, but have no idea how to be there for yourself. Your dreams have been put on hold as you support your husband, children, siblings, and friends in getting their needs met. Finally, you can't stand one more day of neglecting yourself and your own desires. You trace this pattern of behavior back by asking, "What kind of person would go after her dreams and not be there for other people?" The answer you hear is "A selfish person." For a moment you feel happy that you're not that selfish person, because you hate selfish people. Looking back, you remember being told over and over again in religious school how bad it is to be selfish, so you made what you believed to be the right decision—that you would never be that. Instead, you became the opposite—a selfless, big-hearted, loving, and kind person who would do anything for the world—and with that internal commitment, people pleasing became your pattern.

To make peace and break this cycle, you must now confront the distaste you feel for the notion of being selfish and expose the judgments you have held toward all those who you have deemed selfish in the past. You must admit to the negative connotations you attach to the word "selfish" and be willing to see that the way you are interpreting that word is limiting, disempowering, and rigid. You must look to see when you decided or were told that selfish people were bad and wrong. You must become willing to open your heart to the selfish part of you and forgive all those who have reflected back to you that being selfish is bad. You must accept the dualistic view that being human comes with both a healthy dose of selfishness and an equal dose of selflessness. If you are unwilling or unable to find a positive view of being selfish and insist on keeping it in the shadow, you will continue to be held, clinched in the pattern of behavior that has you continue to neglect what is important for your individual growth and the fulfillment of your soul's desires.

To embrace what has kept us trapped, we must muster up the courage to find the gift of our selfish self. If self-neglect is a pattern, being selfish is a vital quality to embrace in order to find our true self. It's great to support others in living their dreams—I happen to do it for a living. But if I could never choose selfish behavior, I would never be able to finish writing a book, because I would always be swayed to answer the phone or support one of the many people who want my help or attention each day. If we can't choose between selfish and selfless, we will be driven to bypass what may truly matter to us at the end of our life. Freedom is being able to choose whoever and whatever we want to be at any moment in our life. If we have to act in a particular way to avoid being something we don't like, we're trapped. We've limited our freedom and robbed ourselves of wholeness. If we can't be lazy or angry, we can't be free. When we are reclaiming these parts of ourselves, it's vitally important to remember that we are doing this to own our true magnificence. It's best said by C. G. Jung: "I'd rather be whole than good."

Taking this journey into the past may feel slightly daunting at first. But the fact is this journey is one of the most rewarding trips we can take. It's intriguing to uncover our shadow, to see how it has taken root, and to catch ourselves before we say something we don't really mean or do something that we will regret. Our shadows are there for us, waiting to offer invaluable insights about ourselves. We can never manage or defeat our self-sabotaging behaviors without embracing the shadows that are driving them. There is no pattern of behavior that can't be broken or changed if we are willing to expose its roots and the emotional upset that caused us to reject the shadow aspect in the first place. When we can compassionately embrace the part of us that has set this behavior in place, we will take back the power over our own actions and break the automatic responses of our unwanted patterns. This process often creates a conundrum because, as human beings, we are designed to want to feel safe, and more often than not, repeating the same old behaviors is what gives us a false sense of safety. It somehow feels easier to repeat the past than explore a different outcome. But to break open a repetitive self-sabotaging behavior, we will have to give up this illusion of a safety net for a moment and be willing to feel what's underneath. And when we find ourselves in the presence of one of our shadow aspects, we will be able to unravel the mystery of our undesirable behavior and cause change to begin.

As we become more and more aware of the fruitlessness of succumbing to the same tired old patterns, we can turn to our courageous self, ask for support, come face-to-face with the shadow part of ourselves that is hidden, and have a heart-to-heart. By becoming intimate with the cast of characters that make up our own internal drama, we can learn to make peace and give support to the life that we want to achieve. On the other hand, if we fail to acknowledge the opposing forces that give rise to these characters, we can easily get caught in the trap of believing a story about ourselves that is only partially true, and we can lose sight of the amazing opportunity to be a fully expressed human being. If we refuse to acknowledge the duality within, we will be trapped, identifying with the character whose voice is the loudest within us, no matter what that character's agenda or mission might be.

THE GIFTS OF OUR SHADOW

The shadow contains essential characters in the script of your life. Your job is to learn from the shadow, to integrate it, and allow it to evolve your thinking and expand the boundaries of your self-created persona. Your challenge is to find its value and to bring the light of forgiveness and compassion so that you can defuse its ability to dismantle your life. Your job is to bring its complex characters out from the shadow, and to use their power and potency as sacred fuel to become who you were meant to be in this lifetime.

If the villain inside you is angry, you must forgive this part of yourself and consider the possibility that anger is exactly what you need to fight against some injustice or oppression or to get you out of an abusive situation and back on track to creating an amazing life. If your shadow is filled with fear about who you are and what you think and masks the real you by creating a phony and inauthentic self, you must forgive yourself and look to see how and where these qualities can be put to use. Maybe these parts of you will help you deal with a controlling partner or a bullying ex-spouse who threatens to destroy your relationship with your children. If the villain in your life story is insatiable and always searching for something to fill its emptiness, you don't need to repress its urge through feeding an addiction and continually beating yourself up. Instead, you can harness the energy of this aspect of yourself and use it to make positive change in your life or the life of someone you care about.

The point is you must forgive yourself for possessing all these human qualities and find a healthy respect and a healthy outlet for each and every aspect of yourself. You never know when you will need a part of you that you have locked away. You never know when a part of yourself that you deemed to be worthless will deliver the exact skill you need to make a difference for yourself or another.

I'm reminded of Jason, a thirty-year-old with rugged good looks and an addiction to all things dangerous. As a young boy, after being labeled by his friends and family members a "scaredy cat," Jason decided that fearful was the last thing he wanted to be. He started playing hockey when he was eleven and soon developed a taste for extreme sports. His love of danger was the perfect cover-up; no one who scales mountains or jumps out of airplanes could ever be accused of being a coward.

After coming home from one of his infamous trips abroad, Jason decided to visit his divorced mother to meet her new fiancé. He was shocked to find out that Jack, the man of his mother's future, was close to twenty years her junior. After Jason had spent an evening listening to Jack dodge questions about his job history and his businesses, Jason's fear overwhelmed his usual respect for his mother's boundaries, and he set out to find out everything about his mother's new boyfriend. An Internet search revealed nothing, so he asked a few acquaintances who were closer to his own age to check into the million-dollar business that Jack had been alluding to all evening.

In a matter of days, Jason's suspicions were validated as he uncovered a recent bankruptcy, a horrible credit history, lawsuits, and a long list of debts. Jack's multimillion-dollar business had a nice office space, but failed to have any business to speak of. Although Jason's suspicions were confirmed, days later he still couldn't muster up the courage to say anything. Then, when his mother announced that Jack would soon be moving in with her to combine household expenses, Jason looked inside to find the strength to voice his concerns, but instead he found only the scared little boy who didn't want to lose his mother's love. His shadow was now dictating what he could and could not say. Jason knew he had to speak up, but felt paralyzed in the presence of his fearful self, which had been banished for all these years. Only by acknowledging and opening his heart to his fearful self—relegated to the shadow—did Jason find the courage to finally tell his mother what he knew. He was able to ask his mother to reconsider having Jack move in until she had found out the truth of who he was. Unattached to the choice she would ultimately make, Jason felt proud that he had the courage to reveal what he knew to his mother and now had a healthy dose of compassion and respect for his fearful self. After all, it was his fearful self, not his courageous self, that had prompted him to unmask the man who was likely preying upon his mother.

Looking further, Jason was able to identify many times that his fearful, suspicious self helped him stay out of trouble. Having found the gifts of his fear, Jason no longer had to play the role of the fearless risk taker all the time. Now he had nothing left to prove. He reclaimed a deep strength he never knew existed when this shadow aspect had remained hidden in the dark.

To be a whole human being, we have to acknowledge the existence of *all* our feelings, human qualities, and experiences and value not just the parts of ourselves that our ego has deemed acceptable, but everything that we have deemed wrong or bad. If we are willing to allow our dark side to be a part of the whole of who we are, we will find it comes equipped with all the power, skill, intelligence, and force needed to do great things in the world.

The journey to extract the gold in the dark, to find the gifts of our shadow demands that we bring radical honesty to the places where we've been in denial; forgiveness and compassion to the parts of ourselves that we've been ashamed of; love and acceptance to the difficult experiences from our past; and courage to the areas of our life where we've been afraid to admit our vulnerabilities. It's not a process of smoothing over, covering up, or pretending that the things we do to sabotage our success are not that big a deal. In fact, only by admitting the cost of some of our behaviors will we unlock the energy to defy the gravitational pull of our past and step into the infinite possibilities of our true self.

When we come face-to-face with the shadow, we soon realize that this part of ourselves is not trying to destroy us. Instead, the shadow self is trying to lead us back to wholeness. I'm reminded of the scene in *Batman: The Dark Knight* in which the Joker is holding a knife to Batman's throat. Batman dares the Joker, "Go ahead and kill me." The Joker, with a perplexed, twisted look on his face, replies, "I don't want to kill you. You complete me." What he is saying is that without his heroic counterpart, he would be nothing at all. If we are savvy enough to enroll our inner villains—our pessimist, our arrogant self, our dictator, our victim—in the script of our highest self and recognize that they are not enemies, but rather hurt and lost parts of ourselves that are in deep need of love and acceptance, we can live in accordance with our soul's highest mission and find peace in this world.

EMBRACING OUR LIGHT SHADOW

Our shadow isn't just our dark qualities or things society considers bad. Our shadow also includes all the positive qualities we've hidden away. These positive qualities are often referred to as our "light shadow." It's not just our darkness we've buried. It's our positive traits—our powerful, loving, and delicious aspects—as well. The fantastic and interesting news here is that we have buried as much of our light as we have of our darkness. We may have buried our genius, competence, humor, success, or courage. Maybe we've hidden our self-confidence, charisma, or power. Maybe our full self-expression, uniqueness, or joyful self was buried after we heard, "Don't be too big for your britches," "Don't brag or people won't like you," or "It's lonely at the top."

We find our hidden light shadow the same way we discover our dark one. We look around for the places where we are projecting our light onto other people. If we see someone we want to emulate, it's because we are seeing qualities that exist within us. If we are enthralled by someone else, it is because the aspect we love in that person exists inside us. There is no quality that we respond to in another that we lack. It might be hidden behind some bad behavior or an old, outdated shadow belief that says we are the exact opposite of what we are seeing in the other person. But I promise you that if you are attracted to a quality in someone else, no matter how great, it also exists inside you.

More than twenty years ago, as I continued making progress in my recovery from drug addiction, my life in South Florida, where I owned a retail boutique, seemed empty and insignificant. I kept feeling the impulse to do something deeper and more meaningful, so I decided to go back to school and study psychology, thinking that I would become a therapist. I had moved to San Francisco and was immersed in consciousness studies and enamored with shadow work. One night my sister called to tell me that Marianne Williamson was speaking at the Palace of Fine Arts. She got me a ticket to the sold-out event, and as I sat in the audience I was stunned. I watched as Marianne boldly called people to a higher vision for themselves and the world. I heard her unabashedly implore us to step out of the smallness of our own ego-centered lives and into the grandness of serving as part of a divine mission. Although I was listening intently to the words she spoke, I was more overcome by her presence. I left there completely in love with Marianne Williamson.

I returned to my apartment, intent to discover the parts of myself that I so clearly saw in her. I loved that she had the courage to speak the truth, even if it meant shocking people in order to wake them up. Also I admired the way she was able to clearly articulate a difficult message, speaking with such eloquence that her words penetrated into people's minds and hearts. I was enamored with the depth of concern she seemed to feel for humanity and the sense that she was dedicated to something larger than just her individual life. I also envied her beauty, her sense of style, and her willingness to look like a hot, sexy woman and not one of the many stereotypical frumpy spiritual teachers. She took the stage looking gorgeous and sophisticated, yet her holiness came through loud and clear.

As a dedicated student of projection, I looked beyond her behaviors and tried to discover the underlying characteristics that gave rise to those behaviors. I asked myself, "What kind of person is able to just be herself on stage?" Clearly, an authentic person. "What kind of person would care so deeply for the rest of the world?" A selfless person. "What is the quality that allows Marianne to speak up, to tell the truth even when it's shocking or scary?" I heard very clearly—a bold person.

I looked at my list of qualities, which read, "bold, authentic, and selfless." None of them were characteristics I owned or acknowledged within myself. Those who know me now may find this hard to believe, but back then I was not somebody who told it like it is. Afraid of losing the approval of those I loved, I skirted around issues and lacked the self-confidence to even stand in front of a room without shaking. I was more concerned with looking good than I was with saying something that would change people's lives. I was more concerned with saying it nicely than with being straight or authentic. Yet I knew that if I saw these strengths in Marianne, the potential for them must exist also within me.

I began practicing being more authentic with people and challenged myself to speak up even when I wanted to be silent. To develop the visionary part of myself, I started my day with a prayer for the world and followed with a daily prayer for myself. To be more selfless, I focused on what I could give rather than what I could get. Marianne's magnificence reflected back to me my own hidden potential. By seeing her light, I literally glimpsed who I could be in the world if I had the courage and the tenacity to acknowledge that the strengths I attributed to her were also my own. This is not to say that they don't exist in her as well; clearly they do. Boldness, authenticity, and selflessness are universal qualities; each one of us has the right to express them in our own unique way.

Before I broke the trance of my light projection on Marianne, I wanted my first book to be as beautiful and poetic as her groundbreaking book *A Return to Love.* But as I surrendered to the unique unfolding of these qualities within me, I realized that I was being guided along a different path. My mission was to be the Champion of the Darkness rather than the First Lady of the Light. This was the divine plan for my life, and I never would have glimpsed it if I hadn't embraced all of my projections.

Taking back our light from those we've projected it onto opens the door to an unimaginable future. I never dreamed that I would one day write a book with Marianne Williamson, that we would become friends, or that we would support one another in the fulfillment of a collective mission. This is what's possible when we take responsibility for the light we see and admire in others. Instead of staying in the trance, we own up to the part of us that is aching to come forth and do the work to own it within ourselves.

Whatever inspires you is an aspect of yourself. Any desire of the heart exists to support you in discovering and manifesting it. If you have an aspiration to be something, it is because you have the potential to manifest the quality you are seeing and the behavior that this quality will bring forth. It will not necessarily be in the exact way that others are expressing the quality, but in your own way.

In my workshops, I always pick a different celebrity and ask people in the audience to share with me what they love most about the person. Recently I chose Bono, and of course I heard at least twenty different qualities that people love about him. One person loved his talent; another raved about his creativity; another, his charisma. Some were enamored with his vision, while others were inspired by his leadership, his selflessness, or his generosity. They each shouted out the quality they attributed to him as though everybody couldn't help but see it and would naturally agree. But this is rarely the case, because each person saw him through the lens of their disowned self that wanted to come out and be embraced. Everyone had different perceptions, because everyone had projected a different piece of their light onto the screen of the man named Bono.

In this example, Bono is serving as a great mirror for all those who follow him to find the hidden aspects of themselves. He gives people the opportunity to take back their own light and find expression for the qualities they see in him. All celebrities have the power and responsibility to *not* actually claim people's projections. In fact when they do, they often get trapped in their own illusional self, which promises to make their own shadow act out. Instead, their job is to reflect the projections back to all those who are transferring their light to them.

Remember, our shadow is often so well hidden from us that it's nearly impossible to find. If it weren't for the phenomenon of projection, it might stay hidden from us for a lifetime. Some of us buried our shadow traits when we were three or four years old. When we project onto other people, we have an opportunity to finally find these buried and hidden treasures.

INTEGRATING THE SHADOW

By now, you might be able to acknowledge that the shadow—with all its pain, trauma, and strife—is an indestructible part of who we all are. No matter how hard we try, we will never succeed in getting rid of it or squelching its presence. We do, however, get to decide if we will allow it to destroy our life and rob us of experiencing our greatness, or if we will milk it for all its wisdom and use it to propel us into the most extraordinary version of ourselves. We have all tasted the sweetness of love, the sour disappointment of loss, the bitterness that remains after a heartbreak. Every one of these experiences is part of our divine, unique recipe. We wouldn't be who we are without them. Most of us suffer from the painful and unwanted parts of our recipe, but there are some extraordinary people who choose to use their pain to heal their heartache and contribute to the world rather than get suffocated by the shadow aspects of their past.

John Walsh, the host of *America's Most Wanted*, did just that. The death of a child is one of the toughest ingredients any one of us could imagine having to survive, yet many will have this experience as part of their recipe. After his six-year-old son Adam was murdered, John became an advocate for victims' rights and turned his anger into action by establishing a television program and advocating for legislation that has led to the prosecution of tens of thousands of criminals. He could have just as easily chosen to swallow his grief or stay a victim himself to this most horrific experience, but instead he chose to use his anger, pain, and heartache to create the television show *America's Most Wanted*, which is responsible for capturing over a thousand fugitives and bringing home more than fifty missing children. Out of the heartbreak of his personal trauma, he was able to save others from experiencing the same pain and has emerged as a man who is awed and respected.

After her only sister died of breast cancer at the age of thirty-six, Nancy Goodman Brinker—a breast-cancer survivor herself—founded the Susan G. Komen Breast Cancer Foundation, a nonprofit that has raised over $1 billion for research, education, and health services. By embracing the events of her life and making a commitment to *not* be a victim, she has done extraordinary things to raise awareness, to help others seek early detection of this potentially life-threatening disease, and to advance the search for a cure.

Can you imagine what our world would look like if Thomas

Edison had not embraced all of himself and his experiences? At a very young age, he had all the evidence in the world to believe that he was a loser, a failure, and an idiot. He tried thousands of different theories for discovering electricity, each of which appeared likely to succeed—and failed each and every time. But instead of giving up, he looked beyond his failures, learned from them, and kept going. He held on to and believed in the possibility of his genius, his vision, even before it had been proven. If he had done what most of us do, if he had labeled himself a loser and stayed trapped within the confines of his limitations, refusing to forgive himself for his failures, we would all still be in the dark—literally. Because Edison was able to integrate and learn from his failures, he found the motivation to continue to pursue success and turn on the lights for all of us.

Edith Eva Eger arrived at Auschwitz on May 22, 1944. After being separated from her father and witnessing her mother being taken away to the gas chamber, Edie lived each day in the most horrific of circumstances, watching other inmates electrocute themselves on the barbed-wire fence surrounding the concentration camp and not knowing when she took a shower whether water would come out or gas. Edie survived the worst circumstances that any of us could imagine, yet if you met her today, you would see a beautifully integrated human being who allowed herself to thrive in spite of—and in some ways because of—her painful past.

She did this by exercising the choices that were still available to her even under these bleak and inhumane conditions. When she was asked to dance for Dr. Mengele, the architect of cruelty who was responsible for the torture and murder of millions of Jews, she closed her eyes and chose to imagine that the music was Tchaikovsky and she was dancing in Budapest to *Romeo and Juliet*. When the German soldiers took her blood twice a week, telling her that it would help them win the war, she chose to tell herself, "I am a pacifist. I am a ballerina. My blood will never help them win the war." She chose to view the guards who held her captive as more imprisoned than she was. She soothed the pain of her mother's death by repeating to herself over and over, "The spirit never dies." She clung to the part of herself that she still had the power to control and refused to allow anything that happened externally to murder her spirit. "If I survive today," Edie told herself, "then tomorrow I'll be free."

Edie, now a gifted and compassionate clinical psychologist and the matriarch of a wonderful family, is clear that by integrating the darkness that was thrust upon her, she exacted the sweetest type of revenge against Hitler. When she was being filmed for *The Shadow Effect* movie, I asked her if she held any anger toward Hitler. She innocently looked me straight in the eye and said, "I wouldn't hold on to any anger toward Hitler. If I did, he would win the war, because I would still be carrying him around with me wherever I went." Edie is a champion of freedom, the carrier of a light that is so great and inspiring that we would all be served if we walked in her footsteps.

It's so easy to get trapped in our hurt and pain and allow our shadow and our history to dictate our future and undermine our well-being. When we hold on to our resentments toward ourselves or anyone else, we bind ourselves to the very thing that has caused us pain by a cord stronger than steel. As my dear friend Brent BecVar shares, refusing to forgive those who have hurt us "is like being a drowning person whose head is being held under water by someone else. At some point you realize that you have to be the one who fights your way back to the surface." The only way to battle heartache and the oppressive nature of our shadow is with forgiveness and compassion. Forgiveness doesn't happen in our heads, but in our hearts. It unfolds when we extract the wisdom and the gifts from even our darkest experiences and emotions. Forgiveness is the hallway between the past and an unimaginable future.

Stories like these demonstrate that we are all living in accordance with a greater plan and that, indeed, everything happens for a reason.

Nothing occurs by accident, and there are no coincidences. We are always evolving, whether we are aware of it or not. Oftentimes this evolution is painful, but the pain serves an important purpose. It is a necessary ingredient in our divine recipe. By feeling the ache of loneliness, our hearts open to receive more love; by overcoming the people and situations that have oppressed us, we realize the depth of our strength. When we are willing to acknowledge that our pain, traumas, and heartaches have in fact equipped us with wisdom essential for our growth, we naturally forgive and even bless those who came into our life to teach us those difficult lessons. Our lives are divinely designed for each one of us to get exactly what we need to deliver our own unique expression to the world.

Our mind may tell us that bad is bad, good is good, and that we can never really be all that we dream of being, but if our shadow could talk, it would tell us otherwise. It would tell us that our brightest light can shine only when we've accepted our darkness. It would reassure us that there is wisdom in every wound. It would show us that life is a magical journey of making peace with both our humanity and divinity. Our shadow would tell us that we deserve better, that we matter, that we are more than we ever dreamed possible, and that there's light at the end of the tunnel.

As we embrace our shadow, we find out that we are living a divine plan, a plan so important, so vital for our own evolution as well as for the evolution of humankind. Like the lotus flower that is born out of mud, we must honor the darkest parts of ourselves and the most painful of our life's experiences, because they are what allow us to birth our most beautiful self. We need the messy, muddy past, the muck of our human life—the combination of every hurt, wound, loss, and unfulfilled desire blended with every joy, success, and blessing to give us the wisdom, the perspective, and the drive to step into the most magnificent expression of ourselves. This is the gift of the shadow.

PART
III

Only Light Can Cast Out Darkness

MARIANNE WILLIAMSON

In a world so filled with tender magic—from sleeping infants to children playing, to lovers smiling, to friendships that last, to flowers blooming, to the violet hope of sunrise, to the fiery magnificence of sunset, to the brilliance of the body, to the fragile glories of nature, to the wonder of animals, to our capacity to forgive, to the mercy of God, to the kindness of strangers, and a list that could go on and on until it's clear that there really is no end to the manifold expressions of love on earth—there is, as well, something else.

And what *is* that?

Why—in a world where we can be moved to tears by a work of art—does there also exist molestation, rape, innocents with slit throats, unjustly held prisoners, starving children, torture, genocide, war, slavery, and all manner of horrific and unnecessary suffering that exists for no other reason than that someone is cruel enough to inflict it or someone else doesn't care enough to stop it? What force exists, in our minds and in our world, that proactively and seemingly inexorably moves to cause the suffering and destruction of living things?

Why, if God is love, does evil exist?

We live in a world of constant juxtaposition between joy that's possible and pain that's all too common. We hope for love and success and abundance, but we never quite forget that there is always lurking the possibility of disaster. We know there is good in the world, but we know that there is something else as well. And we are living at a time when a contest between the two is both intense and intensifying. Whatever it is that leads human beings to hate, to destroy, and to kill has taken on a collective force like never before, as technology and globalization now give it the capacity to not just strike, but to strike us all, together, as one. Never has there been such an urgent need to dismantle this force, whatever it is, that is so contemptuous of love and intent on destroying us all. This is not just a force that seeks to inconvenience us. It is a force that wishes to see us dead.

Yet this force is in fact an antiforce. It does not so much *do* anything, as it gets *us* to do its bidding. It is a place where we have forgotten who we are, and thus act as we are not. It is a darkness that, like all darkness, is not an actual presence, but is rather the absence of light. It is a black hole in psychic space that exists when light is unseen for even a moment. And the only true light is love.

The problem of what to do with this darkness—called by many names but here termed the "shadow"—is a question that has plagued humanity since its earliest beginnings. There has never been, that we know of, a community or civilization on earth in which love prevailed at all times. Yet we continue to dream of it. Such a state, according to certain religions of the world, is called paradise. Certain religious and spiritual texts suggest we have an ancient memory of such a state, though this state was not of the earth at all. It was our spiritual beginnings, a dimension of pure love whence we come and to which we passionately long to return. The fact that we live at times, even most of the time, so separated from this state of pure love is a psychic rupture of such intense proportions as to traumatize us every moment of our lives. Just as the planet moves so fast that we can't even feel we're moving, we're traumatized at such a deep level that we don't even know we're in trauma.

Separated from love, we are separated from God. Separated from God, we are separated from ourselves. And separated from ourselves, we are insane.

In the words of Mahatma Gandhi, "The problem with the world is that humanity is not in its right mind." That is the problem with the world, indeed. There is a place we go into, both individually and collectively, that is the absence of who and what we are and what we are here to do. It is an inversion of our power, a perversion of our identity, and a subversion of our mission on earth.

The problem is this is not so obvious when we are actually there, for it is a place of gross, cosmic confusion. We are prone to feel, when we are separated from love, that our anger is justified, our blaming another is only reasonable, and our attacking someone is in righteous self-defense even when it is not. Either that, or worse. At times, a person—sometimes even whole nations—can become so sucked into the black hole of lovelessness as to be at the effect of its most extreme, even heinous intentions, for this thing, which is actually a no-thing, is not inert. Human consciousness is like a pilot light that never goes off. The problem is it is used to create either a life-producing heat or a life-destroying conflagration. Where there is no love, there is fear. And fear, once it has gripped the mind, is like a vice that threatens to crush the soul.

So that's what it is, this thing we call the shadow. It does not appear, in most of our lives, as a gigantic fire, but simply as a slow burn. It is you when you make the stupid remark, hurting someone you love and possibly ruining a relationship. Or you when you do the stupid thing that sabotages your career. Or you when you pick up the drink, although you know you're an alcoholic and that if you continue doing this it will kill you. In other words, it is the you within you that does not wish you well. It is your shadow, and it can only be eliminated by shining forth your light.

God's love both dwells within us and extends out from us every moment of every day. When we are living in alignment with our true selves as God created us, we receive love constantly and then extend it outward as we have received it. That is what it means to live in the light.

Yet as commonsensical as this sounds, it does not feel like common sense when someone has behaved in a way that seems undeserving of our love. At such a moment, extending our love to that person feels like the wrong thing to do, and withholding our love feels right. That moment—that little bit of unloving thought that seems like just a tiny thing, just a reasonable judgment—is the root of all evil. It is the cornerstone of the shadow's thought system, for it involves a separation from God and a casting of blame. God never withholds love, and we achieve sanity by learning to love as God loves.

Our task, if we are to cast out the shadow, is to learn to think only immortal thoughts, even though we live on the mortal plane. Our higher thought forms will lift the frequency of the planet, and the world will then transform.

But what about now? What makes us forget who we are, thus turning off the light and splitting the world into two separate states—love and fear? It is one thought: that someone is guilty. How we deal with human imperfection is the essential question that decides whether we dwell in the shadow or in light.

God does not look at a person who has made a mistake the same way we do. God does not seek to punish us when we have made mistakes, but to correct us. When we return to our right minds, loving unconditionally and unwaveringly, then the world itself will self-correct.

That does not mean we lose discernment, boundaries, or brain cells. Divine love is not a weakness. God's love is not a gooey love. It's not even always "nice," in a kind of pink, fuzzy way. It involves radical truth telling, the kind of truth that the heart knows even when the mind resists it. It has less to do with style and more to do with substance. There are ways to very sweetly withhold love, putting too much emphasis on a half-baked understanding of the words "positive" and "supportive"; and there are ways to extend love with a kind of harshly realistic honesty that only appears, much later, to have been love at all.

It is time for all of us to get deeply serious about love. In the words of Dr. Martin Luther King, Jr., it is time to inject "new meaning into the veins of human civilization." We need to expand our sense of love beyond the personal, to its social and political implications as well. Only in doing so will we cast out darkness that now hangs like a specter above the world. Living in the darkness, we are living in the shadow. And in the shadow, suffering reigns.

IT MIGHT NOT BE REAL,
BUT IT SURE LOOKS REAL

Sometimes you have a fight with someone you love and you can't even believe it's happening. It feels like a nightmare. You actually hear yourself saying, "This can't be happening!" And that's because it *isn't*—you are lost in a parallel universe, a hallucination of separation and conflict.

Years ago, I told myself not to worry about the Devil, because that was all in my mind. And then I remember what happened next. I simply stood there, stopped in my tracks by the thought that, in fact, that was the worst place it could possibly be. I'm not so much comforted by the idea that there's no Devil out there stalking the planet for my soul, as staggered by the idea that there is an ever-present tendency within my own thinking to perceive without love and thus make myself miserable.

So where did this "tendency" come from? If God is love and love only, and God is all-powerful, then how did a counterforce ever come into being?

The answer, metaphysically, is that actually it did not. Nothing but God's love exists, and in the words of *A Course in Miracles*, "What is all-encompassing can have no opposite." The operative reason for how an illusory world that actually does *not* exist but seems so strongly *to* exist came into being is the principle of free will.

We can think whatever we want to think. Our thoughts, however, have power no matter what we think, because our creative power comes from God. The law of cause and effect guarantees that we will experience the result of whatever it is we choose to think. When we think with love, we are cocreating with God and therefore cocreate more love. When we think without love, however, we manufacture fear. What that means is that we have split minds. One part of us dwells in the light, eternally at one with God's love. Yet another part of us—a part most often aligned with the mortal world—dwells in darkness. And that is the shadow self.

God doesn't see the shadow because, not being love, it does not actually exist. Yet being all-love Himself, He registered our suffering when we fell into the darkness and provided for us an instantaneous healing. In that moment, He created a loving alternative to our self-imposed insanity and fear. This alternative is like a divine ambassador that dwells with us in the world of darkness, always available to lead us back to light, should we request it. This ambassador has many names, from Thought Adjuster to the Holy Spirit. For our purposes here, we will call it the Illuminator.

In *A Course in Miracles*, it is said that we are not perfect or that we would not have been born—but that it is our mission to become perfect here. It is our mission to transcend the shadow and become our true self. The Illuminator acts as a bridge between our shadow self and our light. It has been empowered by God to use all the forces of heaven and earth to lead us out of the darkness back into light. It does so first and foremost by reminding us that the darkness *is not real*. When we are lost in the darkness, our greatest power lies in calling on the Illuminator, whose task is to separate truth from illusion. We do this through prayer, and through willingness. "I'm willing to see this differently" is a sentence that gives the Illuminator permission to enter into our thought system and lead us from insanity back to truth.

A few years ago I went to visit a friend, who already had several close girlfriends at her home when I arrived. One woman in the group had a manner of speaking that seemed to me very grandiose, so much so that every time she spoke I felt as if someone were running fingernails across a blackboard. Obviously my mind was wild with judgment, as I could not understand how someone could possibly be so affected in the way she spoke.

As a seeker on the path, I knew that the problem was not with the woman, but within myself—my own lack of compassion. I inwardly said a prayer and expressed my willingness to see her differently. Almost instantly, or so it seemed to me, one of the other women in the room said to the woman whom I'd been judging so fiercely, "I heard your father is being let out of prison. Is that true?"

As I listened, I heard her story unfold. Although I don't remember all the specifics, I do remember that this woman had been held captive by her own father throughout much of her childhood in the basement of their home. She had eventually been rescued, and her father had gone to jail for many years. Hearing of this woman's suffering, I realized why she spoke the way she did. She literally had no model of a healthy adult persona growing up; she didn't even know how to speak in a natural way and was doing her best to piece together what she considered a normal personality. The same mannerisms that had aroused in me such judgment five minutes earlier now aroused in me deep admiration and compassion. She had not changed, but *I* had. In praying, I had called forth the light. The Illuminator entered into the world of darkness and delivered me from my shadow self, my judgmental self, by giving me the piece of information that would replace my thoughts of fear with thoughts of love.

And where, in this lifetime, had I gotten my tendency to judge so harshly to begin with? From a metaphysical perspective, I was not born with it. We are not born in original sin, or error, but in fundamental and primal innocence.

I seem to have a very powerful birth memory. I can't know of course whether it's actually true, but I've had it for as long as I can remember. I even remember seeing the light fixture that hangs over operating tables, which adds to my feeling that this might be true. According to the memory, I came into this world with an infinite amount of love to give, beyond anything I've allowed myself to feel since.

But this was in 1952, when doctors still thought they were supposed to slap newborn babies to get them to breathe. So just as I felt this extraordinary love beaming out of me to all living things, in the very next moment I felt myself slapped. The doctor, whom I already loved, had hit me. I remember being absolutely and totally confused, hurt, and traumatized. Why would he do that? I just could not believe that this had happened. And then my mind went blank. I descended into whatever I descended into, and that was that.

That memory, or whatever it is, speaks to the question of whether we are born with the shadow. The answer is no, we are born in perfect love. But whoever we are and whatever we have been through, something or someone—often with the best of intentions—casts us into the realm of shadow, and the task of the rest of our lives will be to exit the darkness and return to light.

From that one moment as a newborn—that one traumatic split from love that reenacted within me the separation of all humanity from the love at our core—I would be forever tempted to lose sight of love. Having been denied love, even for a moment, I am now tempted to deny love to others. And the purpose of my life, as it is the purpose of all our lives, is to remember the love within me by remembering its presence in everyone else.

The woman at my friend's house, admirable though she was, tempted me at first to judgment. But I asked for help, and I was given it. As soon as I was willing to see the light in her, my own light returned. And the shadow was gone.

WHERE THERE'S NO LOVE, EXPECT FEAR

Any thought not filled with love is an invitation for the shadow to enter. We are led to believe in the myth of neutrality: that we don't really need to love as long as we don't actively do harm. But every thought either heals or harms. The infinitely creative power of thought guarantees that whatever we choose to think will result in an effect. If I do not choose to love—if I choose to withhold my love at all—then in that moment there is created a psychic void. And fear will rush in to fill the space.

This applies to my thoughts about others and to my thoughts about myself. Having focused on aspects of someone else's shadow, I cannot but enter my own: the angry one, the controlling one, the needy one, the dishonest one, the manipulative one, and so forth. Once I enter the darkness of blame and judgment, I'm blinded to my own light and cannot find my better self.

Or having forgotten the essential truth of my own being—not appreciating myself by appreciating the divine light that dwells within me—I fall easily into the trap of self-destructive behavior. I engage in whatever form of self-sabotage will make others forget, as I have forgotten, who I really am. Whether we are attacking others or attacking ourselves, the shadow provides the temptation to thoughts of destruction and insanity.

The mind in its natural state is in constant communion with the spirit of love. But the shadow, like love, has its ambassadors within us—thoughts that lure us constantly to perceive in a loveless way. "He said he would hire me and he didn't; he is such a bastard." "Her politics disgust me; I can't stand her." "Eat the whole cake; it doesn't matter what the doctor said." "It doesn't matter if you keep that money; they will never know." The world is dominated by thoughts of fear, and we are constantly fortified in our shadow beliefs.

In the absence of prayer or meditation—an experience of shared love between Creator and the created—we are easily tempted to perceive without love, thus entering the shadow zone within ourselves. Whether we are projecting guilt onto others, actually harming another, or engaging in addictive or self-hating behavior that hurts primarily ourselves, the shadow exerts an ugly influence.

Yet why should we be surprised? Most of us wake up in the morning and, in effect, surrender our minds to darkness. The first thing we do is turn on the computer, read the newspaper, or turn on radio or television news. We download thought forms of fear from literally all over the world, allowing our minds, at a time when they are most open to new impressions, to be influenced by the fear-based thinking that dominates our culture. Of *course* we respond from shadow, for all we've looked at is shadow! Of *course* we feel depressed, unhappy, out of sorts, and cynical. The world is dominated by fear-based thinking, and on the mortal plane fear speaks first and fear speaks loudest. There's no darkness to analyze here, so much as light we need to turn on! In order to avoid the clutches of the shadow, we must constantly reach for the light.

The voice of love is called in both Judaism and Christianity the "still, small voice" for God. That is the voice of the Illuminator, and even five minutes of serious meditation in the morning can guarantee that it will guide our thinking throughout the day. How much better this world would be if more of us would cultivate the sacred in our daily lives. Our busyness is often our enemy, making it hard for us to slow down long enough to breathe in the ethers of the spiritual planes. Just as we sometimes sit in front of our computers while a file is downloading, knowing there's nothing we can do to rush the process, so there is no way to simply give a quick nod to love as we rush out the door in the morning and expect the realms of darkness and fear to not invade our day.

In slowing down, we're more likely to cultivate quiet. Our modern lifestyle is too often prey to shadow thoughts for no other reason than that it's too noisy. Too much television, too much computer, too much outer stimulation diminishes the light that is found only in reflective and contemplative thought. Silence is an attitudinal muscle we build up, giving us the capacity to more easily transform the energies conjured up by the shadow self.

Another way to cultivate light is to commune with others in a holy space. In spiritual groups joined in love and devotion—religious or otherwise—a field of love is magnified so that it lifts all members in the group up to a higher vibration. When you are at church, synagogue, twelve-step meetings, or other group meditations, listening to your heart seems natural. Your shadow self seems far away, neither evident nor triggered. The temptation to enter your shadow still exists and needs to be dealt with, but one of the ways the shadow is diminished is by joining with others in the search for light.

When we're with other people who are saying, "I want to listen to my heart, I need to ask what the most loving thing would be, I want to be ethical, I want to hear God's voice," then it becomes easier to live that way. Like any habit, it becomes easier to cultivate when we're around others doing the same. In developing the habits of spiritual practice, you ground yourself in the light of your true being. If you do not so ground yourself, do not be surprised when you say or do things that you later regret.

On an average day in the life of an average person, the number of shadow thoughts that come up is astronomical. We do our best, we try to be good, but our brain is constantly active, and the tendency toward fear-based thought is always there. But the Illuminator is there as well. And the Illuminator is authorized by God to give us whatever help we need.

Talking to my therapist one day, I was sharing with him that I felt in a very negative place. I told him I was in a place of self-loathing.

He asked me, "What is your case against yourself?"

I said, "I hate myself because I'm so negative." I could see the irony, but I couldn't laugh. Or maybe I did.

He suggested that I try something. "Be in the flow of gratitude," he said. "Whenever you are having that kind of negative thought, go into naming all the things you have to be grateful for."

And I found that technique to be very powerful. For hours, I'd been on a rampage of negativity, but as soon as I began the flow of gratitude, it was as though my shadow disappeared the way the Wicked Witch melted when Dorothy threw water on her. And it was the same phenomenon, really. The shadow isn't even real. It just appears so. And as soon as it's exposed to light, then the darkness disappears. The problem, then, was not just the presence of my negativity, but the absence of my positivity! As soon as I filled my mind with gratitude, the shadow trait of self-hatred could no longer exist. In the presence of love, fear is gone.

But let us not underestimate the power of the shadow. It's not enough to just meditate sometimes; we should mediate daily. It's not enough, if you're a recovering addict, to attend a meeting every once in a while; you should attend a meeting every day. It's not enough that we forgive a few people; we must try our best to forgive everyone, for only love is real. If I withhold it from anyone, then I withhold it from myself. And it's not enough to love only when it's easy; we must try to expand our capacity to love even when it's hard.

The shadows that are lurking today, in our own circumstances and around our planet, demand nothing short of sacred illumination if we are to cast them out. And each of us can add to the light by adding to our love. Of course we love our children, but it's no longer enough to just love our own children. We must learn to love the children on the other side of town and the other side of the world. It's easy enough to love those who agree with us and treat us well. We must learn to love those with whom we do not agree and who have not necessarily treated us justly. Just as we work to build up our muscles, we must work to expand our capacity to love.

There is only one thing that can triumph over our lower self, our shadow self, and that is our higher self. And the higher self dwells within the highest love of all: the love of our Creator, in whom there is no darkness, no suffering or fear. It is psychologically unrealistic to underestimate the power of the shadow, but it is spiritually immature to underestimate the power of God. Prayer is not just a symbol; it is a *force*. Meditation is not just something that relaxes us; it is something that harmonizes the energies of the universe. Forgiveness doesn't just make us feel better; it literally transforms the heart. All the powers that emanate from God are powers that will set us free.

To the shadow, the light is an enemy. But to the light, the shadow is nothing. It simply does not exist.

BY THE WAY, IT'S ON THE MOVE

Consciousness is a dynamic, creative energy. It is not inert, it is not stagnant. It is always expanding in whatever direction it's moving.

Love will always build on love, and fear will always build on fear. The shadow is an inexorable drive toward suffering and pain.

Yet how does this thing—which itself is an illusion, which itself has no life—act as though it does? The answer to that is that although fear itself is not real, the power of thought that carries it *is*. Fear is like an explosive device, and thought is the missile on which it rides. The mind is created to be a conduit of the divine, delivering explosions of love, but free will means we can direct it otherwise, should we choose.

Your mind is always either extending love or projecting fear as well as subconsciously planning how to do more of the same. The shadow is your own mind turned against yourself. Just as Lucifer was the most beautiful angel in heaven before he fell and a cancer cell was a normal working cell before it went haywire, the shadow is your own thinking turned in the wrong direction. It is your self-hatred masquerading as self-love. Your shadow is as intelligent as you are, because it is your own intelligence co-opted for fear's purposes. It has all the attributes of life, because it has attached itself to your life. And like all life, it seeks to preserve itself.

Whenever love is near, the shadow becomes particularly active in order to guard against its own demise. It knows that love is its only real enemy. When the shadow senses love, when it senses the light in you, it literally runs for its life. The shadow will try, in whatever way possible, to invalidate, suppress, make wrong the good in you—for it knows that once you remember the light of your true self, it's gone. And so it fights.

Thus the well-known phrase, "Love brings up everything unlike itself." You met someone with whom your soul feels is a sacred connection? Beware, you're likely to do something stupid in that person's presence. You have an extraordinary chance to manifest your dreams? Beware, you're likely to sabotage the opportunity. And that is the shadow: the evil twin of your better self.

Until there is a conscious movement away from fear toward love, the dynamic energy of fear will be acting as a destructive force that takes no prisoners. It can lead to something as seemingly small as an incident in which you say something stupid but harmless or as consequential as an action that could actually ruin your life. We should neither underestimate its power nor doubt its viciousness, for the shadow is on a rampage—sometimes in a slow and long drawn-out fashion and sometimes more quickly—but it is always intentional in the direction of pain.

In Alcoholics Anonymous, it is said that alcoholism is a "progressive disease." What this means is that it will not stay put; if you've got a problem with alcohol today, then you'll have even a bigger problem with it tomorrow unless you deal with it. And its ultimate goal is destruction, even to the point of death. An addiction such as alcoholism isn't just about alcohol; it's about the movement of dark energy, a shadow force that plagues both body and soul. And the reason so many millions of addicts have gotten sober through AA is that the program makes it clear that only a spiritual experience can save them. Only God is powerful enough to overcome the shadow, whatever its form.

When Jesus said, in the Bible, that we should be of good cheer for he had "overcome" the world, the word he chose there is particularly fascinating. He didn't say that he had "fixed" the world. He said that he had "overcome" dark forces, by being lifted to the realm of consciousness where lower thought forms no longer had power to limit him. And that is the shadow's challenge to us: that we reach so high for the light above—the deep sanity of a higher and more loving perspective—that the shadow itself is rendered powerless.

GROUP SHADOWS

We all recognize the shadow when it takes individual form: a person who is angry, controlling, dishonest, violent, and so forth. But sometimes it's just as important to recognize the collective shadow of a group. Groups such as nations are made up of individuals; therefore it's not surprising that the personality characteristics of its members show up in the collective behavior of the group. But what is less obvious is how energy created in a group—whether loving or fearful—is magnified; the energy of two or more minds thinking in the same way is not just the sum of those two. It increases exponentially.

Terrorism is an example. A pathological ideology can spread like a cancer throughout an entire population. Once large enough numbers of people are enrolled in the destructive thought forms that make up the ideology, the force of their combined energy can be truly confounding to even the most technologically advanced purveyors of brute force. The reason this is true is that the actual power of the terrorist threat lies not in its ideological roots, but in the passionate conviction with which so many people are drawn into it. Terrorists have *conviction*, and therein lies their power. Our power to override their destructive intensity lies in our ability to *love* with as much conviction as they show in hate. Hating with conviction, they draw forth more hatred; when we love with greater conviction, we will draw forth more love.

Just as no person is perfect, so neither is any group. The shadow hides itself from the conscious awareness of both individual and collective, posing always as the light, although it is the essence of darkness. A quote from Ralph Waldo Emerson describes the shadow of nationalism when posing as patriotism: "When a whole nation is roaring Patriotism at the top of its voice, I am fain to explore the cleanness of its hands and purity of its heart." It is often when a group is violating its principles the most that it claims to be standing up for them the most enthusiastically. The shadow is sly in the way it covers its tracks, whether using religion as a cover for burning people at the stake or using patriotism as a cover for imperialistic misadventures.

But just as the collective shadow can bring us down, the collective light can bring us up. Any great literature; popular expressions such as fairy tales, films like *Avatar,* and books like the *Harry Potter* series; and obviously, genuine religious or spiritual group practice—all are examples of collective beams of light.

In the movie *Avatar,* the collective shadow of contemporary America is on full display. We see the dangerous marriage of predatory capitalism to the full might of American militarism, an intellectual haughtiness that disallows deference to spiritual principles, an arrogant disregard for the sacredness of the environment, and an imperialistic tendency to take whatever it wants for no other reason than that it wants to. The ugliness of America's shadow gets a full-on spotlight in this passion play of a film. Yet what lifts the story beyond mere finger-pointing to the level of illumination is its perspicacity regarding the light that is never too far from the shadow.

The Illuminator is always poised to provide an alternative to darkness, drawing loving hearts to the scene of the shadow the way red blood cells are drawn to a wound. Yes, there are characters in the film who represent our worst, but there are also characters who represent our best, and that is important. Within every individual as well as every group, the better angels of our nature do exist. Like darkness, they are on the move (notice that angels are always pictured with wings, while the Devil is not). And in the larger scope of things, the light always wins out in the end. In the words of Martin Luther King, Jr., "The moral arc of the universe is long, but it bends toward justice." We can forget the truth, but the universe never does.

Every person and every group of people has a shadow; that does not make us bad. It makes us human. The point is not to hate the shadow, for it is simply our wounded places that need to be healed.

But the point is not to deny the shadow either, for darkness is only dispersed when it is brought to light. We must face the shadow, as individuals and as groups; to do so is not an act of self-hate, but of self-love. True pilgrims are those who face their darkness and surrender it to the power of love; true patriots are those who face the darkness of their nation and surrender it to the power of truth.

Even when we are lost in our shadow, there is a part of us that knows better. Even in a group that displays wrong-minded behavior, there are always individuals who hold out for truth—whether Aryan Germans who hid Jews during World War II at the risk of their own lives or the earthlings who heroically came to the defense of the Na'vi citizenry of Pandora in *Avatar*. There is historical evidence as well as mythical lore that reveal the ultimate triumph of love. The significance of World War II lies not only in the evil of Hitler, but in the brilliance and sacrifice of those who defeated him. The archetypal truth of *Avatar* lies not only in the violence that was done to the Na'vi, but also in how the violence ended. The ultimate point of great religious stories is not the crucifixion but the resurrection, not the slavery of the Israelites but their deliverance to the Promised Land. Now, in our day and age, with so many shadows threatening, it behooves us to remember that shadows appear very dark, but are as nothing before true light.

This truth can be very hard to accept, when all rational evidence points not only to the reality of the shadow, but also to its permanence. The miracle of illumination, however, does not come from rational evidence; it comes literally from "out of the blue," a consummate visual symbol for the realms of pure potentiality. The potential for infinite breakthrough emerges when our proactive embrace of the light is even greater than our fear of the dark.

We cannot perceive that light with the body's eyes. It is a reality that calls for a different kind of seeing. Mortal manifestation is "real," but only immortal love is "Real." In the words of Albert

Einstein when speaking of the physical world, "Reality is merely an illusion, albeit a very persistent one."

If we identify only with the mortal world, then fear does indeed seem justified. But if we extend our perceptions beyond this world, then we see things in a higher and more hopeful light. We see that it's programmed into the true nature of things that love will always reassert itself. Although we are doomed to fall into the shadow—to descend into the psychic underworld of our own unhealed places—we are also guaranteed deliverance. The Illuminator is an eternal presence, active not only within the individual heart, but also within the collective psyche. When individuals humble themselves, asking for forgiveness and correction, then mercy arrives. And the same is true for a group. When German chancellor Gerhard Schroeder apologized to the Polish people for the murder of half a million Poles during World War II, and when Pope John Paul II apologized for the Inquisition, such "purification of memory," as these admissions were described by the late pope, called down a light from the consciousness of heaven and shadows were dispersed.

Individuals are on a path of destiny, and so are groups. Sometimes, we take two steps forward into love and then one step back into the shadow. But the lure of the light is in the final analysis much greater than the lure of the dark.

GOOD INTENTIONS ARE NOT ENOUGH

The modern mind has undeservedly high self-esteem; it is arrogant in its belief that it can simply "decide" what it wants and then make it happen. Yet think of the things that fall away from its grasp: the end to unnecessary suffering, world peace, a healthy planet. Why, in a world so full of genius, does the shadow still lurk and cause the problems it does?

One of the reasons the modern world remains at the effect of the shadow is that it fails to recognize the shadow's metaphysical roots. Evil is an energy, just as love is an energy. It arises from fear, and fear arises from lovelessness. Trying to eradicate darkness only by material means is to deal with it on the level of effect, but not cause. You can cut off a wart, but it will grow back unless its roots are burned out. And the roots of evil are not material.

But there is a difference between nonmaterial energy that is simply mental and the kind that is spiritual. Many people today have an inflated view of the power of "intention." But in fact, as it says in *A Course in Miracles*, your good intentions are not enough. For alcoholics, merely *intending* to no longer drink will not quite do the trick; merely *intending* to be a better spouse is not quite enough, if an actual change in behavior is necessary. Yet sometimes the change of behavior that is called for in life is not so easy to achieve. Mere intention to do better can be overridden by the power of the shadow. The shadow can override our best intentions, and only love can override the shadow.

Love is God, and God is love. Whether people call on God using the name "God" or simply give up all resistance to love—in which case God is present, even if unacknowledged—the divine power of love is the only power great enough to cast out evil. Whether it's the wisdom to know that feeding more of the starving children of the world is one of the best ways to eliminate future terrorist threats, or surrendering our character defects to God for healing and asking that they be removed, there is a deference to the higher power of love without which we cannot overcome the power of fear.

The shadow's lair is not in your conscious mind, but in your subconscious mind. You don't *consciously* decide to do the stupid thing. You don't *consciously* decide to say something that would make your spouse hate you. You don't *consciously* decide to get drunk at your daughter's wedding and ruin everything. "The Devil made me do it" is not as unsophisticated a notion as it sounds. Good intentions make the Devil laugh. But what don't make him laugh are prayer, atonement, forgiveness, and love. Those things make him leave.

Which brings up the question of religion. Why, if religion is a conduit for divine love, does so much evil still lurk in the world and even within its own ranks? How does one of the largest religious institutions in the world come to harbor pedophiles in its priesthood? And the answer of course is that some religion has nothing at all to do with God. In fact, if anything, the shadow—the energetic counterforce to God—loves to play in the fields of religion. It loves to confuse, and it's definitely confusing to the mind when doctrine or dogma based on love is actually a cover for the grossest lovelessness.

If a religious person hates, God is not present. If an atheist loves, then there He is. As it says in *A Course in Miracles*, the line in the Bible that "God shall not be mocked" means that He *isn't*.

When seeking religious discernment, however, it's important to not throw out the baby with the bathwater. The Latin root of the word "religion" is *religio*, which means to "bind back." Real religion—whether it occurs within the context of an organized institution or a more universal spirituality—reconnects us to the truth of who we are, to the love at our core, and to the compassion that heals. The only way to overcome the shadow is to become our true self, and whatever it is that takes us to that place is in its essence a religious experience. For some people, that is an experience at church, synagogue, mosque, or shrine; for some, it is the experience of a spiritual or psychotherapeutic practice; for some, it is the experience of nature; for some, it is the experience of holding their child in their arms for the first time. The point is not what gets us to the experience, but rather what happens to us and within us once we are there. Something changes in us once we have returned to the core of our being, if even just for a moment. It gives us a taste of what's possible, within us and around us. It lifts the veil that shrouds the reality of love, and the extent of our true power. Once we're realigned with our essential nature, we'll have the power to make shadows disappear.

According to *A Course in Miracles*, "miracles occur naturally as expressions of love." Whenever our hearts are open, the darkness is replaced by light. In the meantime—whether it's in a type of medicine that doesn't include a holistic perspective, a religion that doesn't include love, a therapy that doesn't include a higher power, or a relationship that doesn't include a sacred dimension—the shadow will hover around the door until some moment of fear. Then at that point it will steal through the darkness and put a stake through the heart of someone's dreams.

OWNING AND ATONING

No matter how much we understand about the shadow, the point is to get rid of it. But to do this, we must own it first. The solution to the problem of the shadow, in both Jewish and Christian thought, is the principle of atonement. It is the idea that once we have acknowledged our sins and surrendered them to God with true remorse, we are released from their spiritual consequences. ("Sin" derives from an archery term meaning you've missed the mark; the spiritual meaning of the word "sin" is "error.")

Buddha described the law of *karma*, which basically means cause and effect—action, reaction, action, reaction. The principle of atonement means that in a moment of grace, bad karma is burned. Atonement is a kind of cosmic reset button, by which mortal shadow thoughts are undone and replaced by the perfection of love.

In the Catholic religion, the practice of confession is an ongoing experience of atonement, as penitents confess their sins and ask God for forgiveness. In the Jewish religion, the Day of Atonement, or Yom Kippur, is the holiest day of the year. On that day, Jews admit and ask forgiveness for all sins committed during the year leading up to that day; they ask God for the chance to be inscribed for another year in the Book of Life. In Alcoholics Anonymous, addicts are advised to take a fearless moral inventory, admitting their character defects and asking God to remove them. All of these are examples of the spiritual process by which the shadow, when brought to the light, is then transformed through the power of atonement.

Atonement exists because it is necessary. We are all human, we are all wounded, and we all fall prey to the shadow side of human existence. We have all fallen, yes, but we are not without the means to rise back up. In order to do so, however, we must commit to the power that rebuilds our wings. We must be willing to bring our darkness to light and to consciously and willingly surrender it to God.

Let's say I have come to realize that a difficult situation in my life was caused by my own error or personality defect. Perhaps I was controlling in a relationship and so created conflict with a friend or family member. Atonement calls for me to recognize my shadow aspect—in this instance, my controlling nature—and ask God to remove it.

As we've discussed before, it's not enough to just say, "Okay, I won't be controlling anymore." That is certainly a good resolution and may go a long way toward correcting behavior. But when a trait is an actual pattern within your personality—a shadow face you wear that is truly you at your worst or near worst—then it has become entrenched within your attitudinal matrix. It is not enough to just decide to be different, because the shadow has overridden your normal decision-making powers. Once a shadow persona has developed—you the cynical, you the jealous, you the raging—then healing requires that you atone: that you take responsibility for the damage you might have already done and ask God to change your heart.

It is critically important that we look deeply at our own thoughts and actions—particularly where they have been mistaken. In doing so we are addressing not only our individual shadow, but the collective shadow as well. Ultimately, the healing of the world will emerge not from our changing and correcting others, but from our willingness to change and correct ourselves. Since all minds are joined, our ability to self-correct has a corrective influence on the entire universe. In a very real way, it's the only thing that does.

This correction might begin with a nudge from conscience. Conscience is healthy shame—a temporary discomfort that comes not from the shadow, but from the light. It is only a sociopath, after all, who feels no remorse. It is part of what makes us human, that something in us knows when we have been wrong.

The process of atonement involves courage, compassion, and honesty with oneself: "I bring this up. I realize it is my wound. I'm willing to look at it, and I'm willing to change." It is so easy, when a situation is difficult, to cast all blame for the problem onto others. But the true seeker says, "What did *I* do wrong? What was *my* part in this disaster?"

If we don't look at where we're dishonest, harsh, unforgiving, disrespectful, greedy, domineering, and so on, then we cannot change that thing. If we just suppress our shadow, trying to disown it, then it exists as an unintegrated fractal of our personality. And we have no power over what we have not explored. Whatever it is, it will act like an emotional terrorist embedded within our psyche, able to ambush us at any time. It will make itself known in one situation or another as a psychic scream we cannot ignore. This is nature's brilliant way of forcing us to look at something, for nothing gets our attention like going through a personal disaster and knowing that we caused it.

The shadow acts like a series of land mines in your personality. You think you're doing so well—you've got your list together, your organization together, your business plan together, your money together—you think you've got everything so together, and then you go do something that totally blows everything. You can hardly believe it. Nobody else blew it—*you* blew it. And you finally realize that until you deal with that part of your personality, you'll probably blow it again.

I asked a woman once, "Are you in a relationship now?" And she said, "I hate who I am when I'm in a relationship. I'd rather not be in one." So many people can relate. We say to ourselves, "I don't even want to go out there. I don't want to attract a relationship or a business opportunity or whatever, until I have healed whatever part of myself that is sure to sabotage it when and if it happens."

It takes courage to deeply look at ourselves, but we can't have real freedom and peace until we do. That's why we want to be careful not to overemphasize a quick and easy trip to happiness. Enlightenment gets us to joy, but not immediately. First we must face the sorrow that stands in front of it.

We must take the time to reflect on our own dysfunction, our shadows, because unless we look at them, they remain in place. But this can be hard. We heal through a kind of detox process, and sometimes we have to burn through difficult feelings as they come up for review. Something emerges from the shadow of our subconscious mind, giving us the chance to see it clearly, and we are horrified to think we were ever like that. But we are not left at that place without the Illuminator's help. If we so choose, we can surrender our darkness and ask that it be healed. God will not take from us what we do not consciously release to Him, for to do so would be a violation of our free will. But what we do surrender and atone for is then transformed.

Such inner work can be painful, but it is vital and unavoidable. Emotional pain is important, just as physical pain is. If you had broken a leg and it wasn't painful, how would you know it needed to be reset? Physical pain is a way the body says, "Look at this. Care for this. Tend to this." And psychic pain is the same. Sometimes we need to say, "I need to tend to this pain. Why is it here? What is this situation trying to tell me? What part of myself do I need to address?" If you go to the doctor with a torn knee, the doctor doesn't say, "Well, let's look at that elbow." It is the same with God. The wound must be looked at. And the physician, both human and divine, is not there to judge you, but to heal you.

We're often afraid of taking a good look at our shadow, because we want to avoid the shame or embarrassment that might come along with admitting our mistakes. We feel if we take a deep look at ourselves, we'll be too exposed. We don't want to look at our own shadow, because we're afraid of what we might see. But the only thing we should actually fear is *not* looking at it, for our denial of the shadow is exactly what fuels it.

At first you say, "I don't want to look at it, because I'll hate myself." But then you say, "No, I have to look at it, because otherwise I can't release it to God." And something counterintuitive and wonderful happens when you do. One day I looked at something in myself that I had been avoiding because it was too painful. Yet once I did take a look, I had an unexpected surprise. Rather than feeling self-hatred, I was flooded with compassion for myself, because I realized how much pain I would have had to be in to develop that sort of coping mechanism to begin with.

All of us are scarred, yet the problem is that our scars don't show up as such in the eyes of other people. Rather, they show up as character defects. If a three-year-old is screaming and crying, we're likely to say, "Oh, the poor darling is so tired." But when you're a crying and screaming forty-year-old—even if your pain is directly related to your trauma as a three-year-old—people don't say, "Oh, he's so tired." They say, "He's horrible."

Your character defects are not where you're bad, but where you're wounded. But no matter who or what caused the wound, it's yours now and you're responsible for it. The only person who can bring it up and release it is you. Ultimately, it doesn't matter where you got your character defects anyway. They're yours now. You can't live with a sign around your neck saying, "It's not my fault. My parents were difficult." Your only way out of your conundrum is to take total responsibility for those defects.

Your character defects are the way you self-sabotage, the way you hurt yourself and others. That's why you have to look at them. Until you take complete responsibility for your own experience, you can't change it. But once you've truly looked at yourself, you can start healing. You've opened your eyes and now you see. "I see that I did that. I admit it. I get it. I atone for my error. I am willing to make amends. I am willing to make it right. And I pray to become a better person now."

In the moments when you acted out of your shadow, you didn't wake up that morning and say, "I think I'll be a jerk today." You didn't go into a meeting and say, "I'm going to say and do things that make people reject me." No, in those moments, you didn't realize you were doing it. You were at the effect of the shadow. The shadow cast you into darkness, and you were blinded to the light. And so you suffered.

The shadow leads us to do something stupid and then punishes us savagely for having been so dumb. The shadow has no mercy, but God does. Hell is what the shadow creates here, and love is what delivers us from it. Atonement is an aspect of God's love. As we atone, we are freed from our dysfunctional patterns and the trajectory of events they produced. This is the miracle of personal transformation. Having delivered our wrong-minded past decisions to God, we can say, with a line from a prayer in *A Course in Miracles*, "I will not feel guilty, for the Holy Spirit will undo all consequences of my wrong decision if I will let Him." Once you atone with a sincere and humble heart, you are released from the karmic maelstrom of your shadow drama.

Once we have owned who we are in the shadow, we can continue our journey back into the light. We don't heal by pouring pink paint over our issues, pretending they're not there or blaming them all on other people. We heal by knowing that whatever shadows hide our light are headquartered inside our own minds. It is our responsibility to admit that they're there, open the door to God, and let Him shine them away. He always has, and He always will.

FORGIVE YOURSELF, FORGIVE THEM

Someone might have hurt you fifteen years ago, and you're still not shutting up about what that person did to you. But if you're honest with yourself, you might have hurt someone else fifteen years ago and you haven't even looked at it for the last fourteen. We're very big on seeing what other people did to us, but we're not so big on looking at what we might have done to others.

The shadow has no problem focusing on the shadow—as long as it's the shadow in other people! "That person is acting out of his shadow, and that person is acting out of her shadow, and all those other people are acting out of their shadow—but me? What shadow?" More damage is inflicted by people who think they have it all together than by people who have been humbled by the realization that they probably do not. People who have looked deeply into the shadow know that it's not just a little thing or a trivial mistake— it's a cosmic counterforce to the goodness of the world, and it takes any opportunity presented it to wreak havoc on the human heart. Nothing is a greater opportunity for the shadow than our thinking that all our problems lie in other people.

A projection of guilt onto others is endemic to the mortal world.

From the moment we're born, we're taught a belief system that reinforces our sense of separateness: "I'm in my body, and you're in yours. And God is outside us both." More fractured perception emanates from our sense of separation than from any other thing.

First of all, if I'm separate from God, then I am separate from my source, and I feel traumatized the way a baby is traumatized if ripped away from the mother. This trauma induces fear, and I am then likely to be triggered by any person or situation that seems to be taking from me what I think I need—even if that's not the case. My shadow would likely manifest as paranoia or neediness.

Second, if I'm separate from the rest of the world, then I feel powerless, given that I am so small and the world is so huge. This sense of separation leads me to believe that I am weak, when in fact, as a child of the divine, I have infinite resources of strength within. My shadow would then likely manifest as my playing small and being too fearful to stand in my own strength.

Third, if I'm separate from other people, then I am separated from the experience of love and unity that is my birthright as a human being. I cannot help but feel a deep existential loneliness instead of the joy that I am meant to feel in the company of other people. My shadow would likely manifest as either overattachment or under-attachment to others, a superiority or an inferiority complex, manipulative behavior, defensiveness, or a domineering or controlling personality.

Last, all of the above aspects of separation involve a sense of separation from self, from which all other forms of shadow emerge. If I am separate from myself, and my true self is love, then I am separate from love. My shadow would likely manifest as anything seemingly not-love toward myself or others, from substance abuse to violence.

Since all shadow manifestations are rooted in thoughts of separation, then healing the mistaken thought that we are separate from the rest of life—from our Creator, from other people, and from other created things—is the ultimate solution to the problem of the shadow. This reconciliation of mind and spirit, the soul's return to its divine knowing, is the point of illumination that casts out all darkness.

And what is the light we see, when our minds are reconciled to truth? We see not only that we are one with others, but also that all of us carry seeds of the divine. We were created by God, in the image of God, in the likeness of God. We are perfect, as all His creations are. We deserve from ourselves and from each other the same mercy that God shows to each of us. And when we remember this—when our minds are healed of the delusion that our shadows define us—then showing mercy and forgiveness comes naturally.

What is important is not the form your shadow takes. The point is that your shadow developed for one reason and one reason only. In a moment, love left—or so you thought it did. It doesn't matter if it left in the form of a mother's abandonment or a father's anger. What matters is that in that traumatic, primal moment you lost conscious contact with the experience of God's love. And you went temporarily insane. Now, every time that trauma is triggered, you go insane again. The issue is not what caused the trauma. It doesn't ultimately matter what mortal drama led up to it. What matters is that your spirit be restored. What matters is that you reconnect with love *now*, that your mind be healed of its insanity *now*, that you forgive yourself and others *now*.

Forgiveness does not mean that you see the darkness, but then give it amnesty. Rather, it means that you see the darkness, but then choose to overlook it. And you overlook it not because you are in denial, but because you know that the shadow is not real. There is negative denial, and there is positive denial. You are simply denying what is not there.

When you are needy, that is not the real you. When you are acting out, that is not the real you. When you are angry, that is not the real you. The real you is a divine, loving, and changeless being. It can become temporarily invisible, hidden behind a shadowy veil, but it cannot be uncreated, because God created it. It is always there.

The shadow is an illusory self, the mask of an imposter. It has "real" effects within the mortal world—from sabotaging yourself to repelling others—but forgiveness means extending your perception beyond the real to the Real, beyond mortal darkness to the eternal light. And when you see that Reality, in yourself or others, you gain the power to invoke it. We heal when we feel forgiven. We heal in the presence of compassion. If you really want someone to change, the miracle lies in your ability to see how perfect they already are.

The shadow does not leave when it is attacked; it heals when it is forgiven. We do not take off our shadowy mask in the presence of someone who blames us, but rather in the presence of someone who says through words or behavior, "I know this is not who you are." We miraculously heal in the presence of someone who believes in our light even when we are lost in our darkness. And when we learn to see others in the light of their true being, whether they are showing us that light or not, then we have the power to work that miracle for them.

Forgiveness is an action, but it springs from an attitude. It can be difficult to forgive someone whose behavior has hurt us, unless we have grounded our perceptions in a constant effort to see beyond the darkness of the personality.

Spiritual practice is key to our power as light-bearers, for we cannot extend peace if we do not cultivate it. Our thoughts and attitudes need persistent training in a world so intent on convincing us that we are who we are not and that we are not who, in fact, we are. The thinking of love is completely opposite the thinking that dominates this world; that is why we must be constantly *reminded* of the light. Just as you take a shower or bath in the morning to get yesterday's dirt off your body, you do your spiritual practice in the morning to get yesterday's thinking off your mind and heart.

The world is constantly luring us into thoughts of fear rather than love—attack, defense, anger, judgment, and so forth. It would constantly convince us that the shadow is real and that the light is not. "That person *is* a jerk. That person *is* to blame. That person *is* guilty." Or, conversely, "*I* am a jerk. *I* am to blame. *I* am guilty." Yet projecting guilt onto yourself is ultimately no less blasphemous than projecting it onto others.

Real forgiveness means knowing that no one is actually guilty. All of us are innocent in the eyes of God. It is our light and not our darkness that is real.

"RESIST YE NOT LOVE"

Given that Buddha was enlightened under the Bodhi tree and paved the way for a life of compassion, given that Moses simply touched the sea and it parted, given that Jesus was resurrected and rose above death, you'd think we would take those things more seriously. You'd think we would apply their messages more consistently, opening our hearts, parting some waters, and rising above some illusions of our own.

Although billions of souls profess belief in the religions of the world, there is an evolutionary step we seem not yet to be taking. Humanity stays stuck in the shadow, despite all the beings of light and the messages of love that have emerged throughout our history. The great enlightened masters and teachers are our evolutionary elder brothers, beings who've actualized the divine light that resides inside us all. Every religion is a door to that light, and still the door remains too often closed.

And why is that? Why, given the suffering that the shadow imposes, do we not embrace more seriously the light?

In my book *A Return to Love*, one paragraph seems to have struck a chord with people. There is a sentence in that paragraph that I believe is the reason: *It is our light, not our darkness, that most frightens us.*

A big "Bingo!" seems to come up for many people when they read that line. We realize that our problem, if we're honest with ourselves, is not so much that we are imprisoned by the shadow, but that we avoid the light. We actively resist the emergence into our better self. And as long as we don't deal with that, then the pattern of avoidance goes unquestioned and unchallenged. The only way we can escape the shadow is to outgrow it, to drop it like the set of old and outworn clothing that it is, and become the spiritual giants we are intended to be.

Bizarre though it might seem, our shadow is a comfort zone. As long as we are being weak, we bear no responsibility for being strong. We don't owe it to anyone to shine as long as we remain shrouded in darkness. Our emotional habit is to avoid the light. We might say we're waiting for the light to shine on us, but it can't shine *on* us, because it's not shining *from* us.

Somewhere deep inside, we know this. *Our deepest fear is not that we are inadequate. Our deepest fear is that we are powerful beyond measure.* We are standing on the brink of a huge step forward into the light of our true being, not just as individuals, but also as a species. And yet we still hold back somehow. In a final moment of "Shall I, or shall I not?" we are actually pretending to ourselves that we have a choice.

What is your alternative to getting clean and sober—that you die of the disease? What is your alternative to forgiveness—that you become bitter and hard? What is our alternative to seeing the sacred in nature—that we destroy the earth? What is our alternative to peace—that we blow up the world?

The shadow would actually say yes to those things, with a classic repertoire of the insidious and insane. "Have another drink; it's no big deal." "Never forget how much that hurt." "The poor will always be with us." "The earth will be okay; don't worry." And the best one yet for the age we live in: "What, are you soft on terrorism or something?"

There is a magic that happens when you simply say no. "No, I don't wish to be weak anymore. No, I don't wish to act stupidly anymore. No, I don't wish to be known for my defects. No, I don't wish to waste my talents anymore. No, I don't wish to play small anymore."

And there is magic as well when we learn to say yes. "Yes, I will make a choice to love, and I will make that choice each and every day. Yes, I devote myself to the light, and I proactively choose to serve it. In a "sacred marriage" to the divine beloved, I not only commit to higher possibilities and perspective, but—equally important—*I forsake all others.* Of course you *could* become cynical. Of course you *could* become bitter. Of course you *could* just go along. The point is you don't *choose* to anymore.

We ask ourselves, Who am I to be brilliant, gorgeous, talented, and fabulous? Actually, who are you not to be? You are a child of God. Your playing small does not serve the world. There's nothing enlightened about shrinking, so that other people won't feel insecure around you. We were born to make manifest the glory of God that is within us. It's not just in some of us; it's in everyone. And as we let our own light shine, we unconsciously give other people permission to do the same. As we are liberated from our own fear, our presence automatically liberates others.

We have reached a point where humanity is going to travel in one direction or another. We are being forced to choose a path of fear or love. We are moving toward the darkness, or we are moving toward the light. We know what the path of fear would offer. If attack thoughts reach a high enough pitch—let's say, a few hundred nuclear bombs lobbed around the world—then the insanity of the shadow would finally be assuaged. For all would then be dark.

And what about the path to love? What would a world of light look like, were our physical eyes able to see it at all?

I once had a dream I will never forget. I walked into a room that was much like a large restaurant. Everyone there turned around to enthusiastically greet each new person who arrived. In the middle of the room was a gigantic, sparkling fountain, and around the walls people were sitting in booths made to look like large white swans. The other colors in the room were blue, green, and turquoise. The people at every table were deeply engrossed in the most joyful conversations. It was the happiest environment I could ever imagine.

When I woke up, my first thought was that that must be heaven. I looked at the dream that way until I read in *A Course in Miracles* that the line "heaven and earth shall pass away" means that they will no longer exist as two separate states. The point of that dream was not what heaven will look like, but what earth will look like. We will live on earth—as our evolutionary elder brothers did—and yet, like them, think only the thoughts of heaven. We will live on earth, but know a heavenly joy. We will live in a world now saturated with fear, but the light within us will shine so brightly that the darkness shall be no more.

I believe most of us believe, deep down, that we *can* rise up and become the people we are capable of being. We *can* actualize our divine potential. We *can* cast out all shadows through a passionate embrace of light. We *can* become a species of such light-filled consciousness that in our presence all darkness automatically disappears.

We can. And this is not a dream. As any one of us at any time chooses love over fear, we add to a great wave of love that is washing over the world even now. For the sake of the newborn and the flush of new love, for the glory of nature and the wonder of animals, for the mercy of God and the sake of our grandchildren, to honor the sunrise and preserve the sunset—it's time.

The Shadow Effect Test

"It's only when we have the courage to face things exactly as they are without any self-deception or illusion, that a light will develop out of events by which the path to success may be recognized."

—*I Ching*

1. How long have you been working on the same issues, be they in the area of your career, health, intimate relationships, or finances?

    A. Less than twelve months

    B. One to three years

    C. More than five years

    D. More than ten years

2. In the past twelve months, how many times have you misplaced something important, gotten a traffic ticket, had an accident, or destroyed something of value?

A. None

B. Once or twice

C. More than five times

D. More than ten times

3. How often do you feel phony, inauthentic, or find that it takes a lot of effort to get people to perceive you in a certain way?

A. All the time

B. Occasionally

C. Almost never

D. Never

4. If your friends, coworkers, and family members were interviewed, would they say that you complain . . .

A. Seldom to never

B. Maybe once a day

C. Frequently

D. All the time

5. In the past twelve months, how many times have you said something or done something that you later regretted, whether immediately or over time?

A. None

B. Once or twice

C. More than five times

D. More than ten times

6. After you've achieved a personal goal—reached your desired weight, paid off your credit cards, organized your home or office, etc.—which of the following emotions are you more likely to experience?

    A. Relieved that you made it but wary that you may backslide into old behaviors

    B. Entitled—you deserve a reward for all your hard work!

    C. Inspired by your success and committed to keeping up the good work

    D. Resentful that you had to work so hard in the first place

7. How often do you notice yourself feeling inadequate, not good enough, unloved, or unworthy?

    A. All the time

    B. Occasionally

    C. Almost never

    D. Never

8. On a scale of 1–10, how willing are you to speak your truth, even if it runs contrary to the opinions of others?

    A. 8–10; I am very willing to speak my truth.

    B. 5–7; Most of the time I am willing to speak my truth.

    C. 3–5; I am occasionally willing to speak my truth.

    D. 1–2; I am almost never willing to speak my truth.

9.   What is the primary focus of your life right now?

    A.   Advancing your career, improving your health, building wealth, or deepening your relationships

    B.   Managing strained relationships or "putting out fires" at work and at home

    C.   Making measurable progress toward your goals over a reasonable period of time

    D.   Trying to avert or avoid immediate disaster in the area of your finances, relationships, health, or career

10. What percentage of the time can you count on yourself to keep your word and uphold your promises—whether to yourself or to another?

    A.   Less than 10%

    B.   Less than 25%

    C.   About 50%

    D.   Most of the time

11. How much time each day do you spend gossiping—whether talking about someone you know, reading tabloids, or watching gossip TV?

    A.   None

    B.   Less than one hour a day

    C.   More than one hour a day

    D.   More than three hours a day

12. Which of the following statements would you use to describe your life?

   A. Most of the time, things work out fairly easily for me.

   B. I have many talents and gifts, but do not use them to their fullest potential.

   C. I am riddled by bad luck and find myself in one bad situation after another.

   D. I have to work hard just to maintain the status quo.

13. How much time a day do you spend working toward your long-term goals?

   A. None

   B. Less than twenty minutes per day

   C. An hour or more per day

   D. You have no long-term goals

14. How frequently do you feel mistreated, misunderstood, or taken advantage of—in either your personal or professional life?

   A. Every day

   B. Frequently

   C. Occasionally

   D. Seldom to never

15. When asked to do something that you have no interest in doing, you are most likely to . . .

   A. Say no with a clear conscience

B. Say no but feel guilty about it

C. Say yes but not follow through

D. Say yes, do it, but feel resentful about it

16. Imagine that your life is a house with many rooms—some you like, some you feel ashamed of. How many people do you allow to see *all* of your rooms?

A. Nobody

B. One significant person—a spouse, lover, best friend, parent, etc.

C. A small handful of people know me that well

D. There are many people in my life who know me that well

17. When you feel hurt by someone or something, what do you tend to do?

A. Keep it to yourself

B. Reflect, forgive, and move on

C. Confront the situation head-on

D. Talk about it to everyone but the person involved

18. When you get an impulse or an idea about how to improve some aspect of your life, what do you do?

A. Ignore it completely

B. Take a few steps in the right direction but rarely see the project through to the finish line

C. Tell yourself that "I'll get to it one of these days"

D. Create a support structure around yourself to ensure that you take action

19. The last time you found yourself with a block of unexpected free time, what did you do?

A. Squandered it by catalog shopping, watching TV, or surfing the Internet

B. Used the opportunity to move forward on an important project

C. Relaxed and rejuvenated yourself by taking a nap, meditating, or reading

D. Your life is so hectic that you can't recall an occasion when you had an unexpected block of free time

20. When you make a mistake, what are you most likely to do?

A. Be gentle with yourself and resolve to do things differently in the future

B. Put things in perspective by acknowledging yourself for what you did right

C. Fall into a downward spiral of self-criticism

D. Interpret your misstep as evidence that you are incompetent, and stop trying

CALCULATING YOUR SCORE:

Below, circle which answer you chose for each question.

Question I
A = I, B = 3, C = 5, D = 8

Question 2
A = I, B = 3, C = 5, D = 8

Question 3
A = 5, B = 3, C = I, D = 0

Question 4
A = 0, B = I, C = 3, D = 5

Question 5
A = 0, B = I, C = 3, D = 5

Question 6
A = 0, B = 5, C = 0, D = 3

Question 7
A = 5, B = 3, C = I, D = 0

Question 8
A = 0, B = I, C = 3, D = 5

Question 9
A = 0, B = 3, C = 0, D = 5

Question 10
A = 8, B = 5, C = 3, D = I

Question II
A = 0, B = 3, C = 5, D = 8

Question 12
A = 0, B = 3, C = 5, D = 3

Question 13
A = 5, B = 3, C = 0, D = 5

Question 14
A = 5, B = 3, C = I, D = 0

Question 15
A = 0, B = 3, C = 3, D = 5

Question 16
A = 5, B = 3, C = I, D = 0

Question 17
A = 5, B = 0, C = I, D = 5

Question 18
A = 5, B = 3, C = 3, D = 0

Question 19
A = 5, B = 0, C = 0, D = 3

Question 20
A = 0, B = 0, C = 5, D = 5

Total Score = _____ (calculate by adding up the answers you circled)

Then turn to the next page to discover how *the shadow effect* is at work in your own life.

THE SHADOW EFFECT ASSESSMENT:

If you scored 3–37 points: You are in the neutral zone, which means that you are free (for now) from many of the internal beliefs and wounds that give rise to destructive behaviors caused by your shadow. You have high self-esteem, your actions are closely aligned with your values, and you are most likely making great forward progress toward your long-term goals. Keep on loving and listening to yourself.

If you scored 38–75 points: You may not be experiencing the full weight and impact of the shadow at this moment, but you are likely expending a lot of effort to repress and hide parts of yourself and your life that you do not like. The energy you are using to keep things from spinning out of control—whether at work, at home, or with your health and well-being—would be put to better use if it were directed toward achieving your goals and desires.

If you scored 76–112 points: Either you spend a lot of time and energy trying to manage other people's opinions of you, or you are deeply resigned about the conditions of your life. This is the shadow at work and it paralyzes you from taking corrective actions. If left unchecked, the internal chaos you are experiencing may lead you on a crash course for disaster. The good news, however, is that every act of self-sabotage presents an opportunity to awaken you to what is truly important. Open your heart, explore the shadow, and you'll begin to see how your deepest pain, when digested and understood, is designed to lead you to your greatest destiny.

—

Shadow work is the work of the heart warrior. If you're ready for more love, more peace, more satisfaction, and more success, visit us at www.TheShadowEffect.com.

About the Authors

DEEPAK CHOPRA is the author of more than fifty-five books translated into over thirty-five languages, including numerous *New York Times* bestsellers in both fiction and nonfiction categories. Some of his bestselling books include *The Seven Spiritual Laws of Success; How to Know God; The Spontaneous Fulfillment of Desire; The Book of Secrets; Buddha; The Third Jesus; Jesus; Reinventing the Body, Resurrecting the Soul;* and *The Ultimate Happiness Prescription.*

Chopra's *Wellness Radio* airs weekly on Sirius XM Stars, channels 102 and 55, and focuses on the areas of success, love, sexuality and relationships, well-being, and spirituality. He is a columnist for the *San Francisco Chronicle* and *The Washington Post* and contributes regularly to Oprah.com, Intent.com, and The Huffington Post.

Dr. Chopra is a fellow of the American College of Physicians, a member of the American Association of Clinical Endocrinologists, adjunct professor at Kellogg School of Management, and senior scientist with the Gallup Organization. *Time* magazine heralds Deepak Chopra as one of the top one hundred heroes and icons of the century and credits him as "the poet-prophet of alternative medicine."

Please visit the author at www.deepakchopra.com.

DEBBIE FORD is an internationally acclaimed teacher, speaker, transformational coach, filmmaker, and bestselling author who has guided tens of thousands of extraordinary people to learn to love, trust, and own all of who they are.

Debbie is a pioneering force in incorporating the study and integration of the human shadow into modern psychological and spiritual practices. Debbie is the executive producer of *The Shadow Effect* movie, an emotionally gripping, visually compelling transformational documentary featuring Deepak Chopra, Marianne Williamson, and other provocative thinkers and beloved teachers. The film has been recognized at prestigious film festivals and has been lauded as one of the most important movies of the decade. Debbie is the author of the number one *New York Times* bestseller *The Dark Side of the Light Chasers* as well as *The Secret of the Shadow* and *Why Good People Do Bad Things*. She is also the creator of the world-renowned Shadow Process Workshop.

Debbie is the founder of The Ford Institute for Transformational Training, the renowned personal and professional training organization that offers emotional and spiritual education to individuals and organizations around the world based on her body of work on the shadow as well as her books *Spiritual Divorce, The Right Questions, The Best Year of Your Life,* and *The 21-Day Consciousness Cleanse*. Her passion and dedication to education also inspired her and the global community of transformational coaches she has trained to create The Collective Heart, a nonprofit organization helping to transform education around the world.

Visit Debbie at www.DebbieFord.com.

MARIANNE WILLIAMSON is an internationally acclaimed spiritual teacher. Her latest book, *The Age of Miracles,* hit number two on the *New York Times* bestseller list. Among her other nine published books, four of them—including *A Return to Love*—were number one *New York Times* bestsellers. *A Return to Love* is considered a must read of the New Spirituality. A paragraph from that book, beginning "Our deepest fear is not that we are inadequate. Our deepest fear is that we are powerful beyond measure"—often misattributed to Nelson Mandela's inaugural address—is considered an anthem for a contemporary generation of seekers.

Marianne's other books include *Everyday Grace, A Woman's Worth, Illuminata, Healing the Soul of America, The Gift of Change,* and *Emma and Mommy Talk to God.*

She has been a popular guest on television programs such as *The Oprah Winfrey Show, Larry King Live, Good Morning America,* and *Charlie Rose.*

Marianne is a native of Houston, Texas. In 1989, she founded Project Angel Food, a meals-on-wheels program that serves homebound people with AIDS in the Los Angeles area. Today, Project Angel Food serves over a thousand people daily. Marianne also cofounded The Peace Alliance, a grassroots campaign supporting legislation to establish a U.S. Department of Peace.

In December 2006, a *Newsweek* magazine poll named Marianne Williamson one of the fifty most influential baby boomers. According to *Time* magazine, "Yoga, the Cabala and Marianne Williamson have been taken up by those seeking a relationship with God that is not strictly tethered to Christianity."

She can be reached at www.marianne.com.